Discovering
the Mass

A Benedictine monk

Discovering the Mass

The Saint Austin Press
MCMXCIX

THE SAINT AUSTIN PRESS
296 Brockley Road
London   SE4 2RA
Tel   +44 (0) 181 692 6009
Fax +44 (0) 181 469 3609

Email: books@saintaustin.org
http://www.saintaustin.org

From the original French:
Découvrir la Messe, 1996, Éditions Sainte Madeleine

Translated into English by Jean Pierre Pilon
and first published in serial form in the American newsletter
of the Priestly Fraternity of St. Peter.

English edition © 1999, The Saint Austin Press

Cum permissu superiorum

A catalogue record for this book is available from the British Library.

ISBN 1 901157 06 7

Designed and printed by NEWTON Design & Print

FOREWORD

The pages which follow first appeared in *La Nef*, a French Catholic journal, between 1992 and 1996, and were subsequently published as a book, *Découvrir la Messe*, by the Abbey of Le Barroux. The monks of Le Barroux celebrate the traditional liturgy and have the status of an Abbey *sui juris*, depending directly on the Holy See. The English translation was first published in the American newsletter of the Fraternity of St. Peter, a society of apostolic life erected by the Holy See. They also have a mandate to celebrate the liturgy according to the traditional rites.

Since the publication of the Motu Proprio *Ecclesia Dei* by the Holy Father, the number of lay people interested in the traditional liturgy (by this, we mean the forms of worship in use throughout the Roman Church up until Advent 1969) has increased significantly.

This is a particularly marked trend amongst the young, many of whom have grown up without experiencing Latin liturgy. It is because of these developments that The Saint Austin Press, in collaboration with the monks of Le Barroux and the Fraternity of St. Peter, has felt it opportune to present this book to the English reading public.

There is much talk these days of a 'crisis in the liturgy' (Cardinal Daneels), of a 'reform of the reform' (Cardinal Ratzinger). In the context of this debate, this little book offers the response of the monks of Le Barroux. It is a simple response: the author unfolds, calmly and clearly, the rich heritage which has been transmitted to us in the traditonal Roman Mass, and which his community is happy to live by to this day. It is a liturgy which has much of value to teach to the people of our age, principally because it underlines so well the *sacrificial* nature of the Mass.

In the first part of this book, time is given to some essential points of doctrine: What is a sacrament? What is the Mass?

What is the liturgy? Then the author comments on the rites as they unfold, explaining their origin and meaning.

It is our prayer that this book will in some measure help the faithful to appreciate and more profoundly to love the Mass, and so contribute to a deepening of what Pope St. Pius X called "that true Christian spirit" whose "indispensable fount ... is the active participation in the holy mysteries and in the public and solemn prayer of the Church."

With this intention, we renew the call made by Dom Prosper Guéranger over 150 years ago: "Open your hearts, children of the Catholic Church, and come and pray the prayer of your Mother!"

London, the Feast of the Annunciation, 1999.

CONTENTS

ON EARTH AS IT IS IN HEAVEN

THE ENTRANCE RITES

THE LITURGY OF THE WORD

THE OFFERTORY

THE SACRED MYSTERIES

THE COMPLETION OF THE SACRIFICE

ON EARTH AS IT IS IN HEAVEN

What could be more delightful than to
imitate on Earth the dances of the angels?
Saint Basil

I

THE SACRAMENTS

Before taking on a step-by-step study of the Mass, it is important briefly to recall what the Mass is, and also the place it holds in the life of the Church.

It was, in fact, our Lord who instituted the Mass so that the work of justification, which He had begun Himself while dwelling among us, would be perpetuated until the end of time. "Behold, I am with you until the consummation of time." He is with us through His Church, which is Jesus Christ extended and communicated through time and space. It is primarily through the sacraments that we are put into intimate contact with His sanctifying power.

What is a sacrament?

A sacrament is a perceptible sign, instituted by Jesus Christ, which makes present the grace that it signifies. Let us study what that means.

A perceptible sign. Saint Paul defines it in baptism, as follows: The *cleansing by the laver of water in the word of life* (Eph. 5:26). The perceptible sign is therefore exactly that: a sacred word ("I baptise you, in the name of the Father, of the Son, and of the Holy Spirit") which is called the *form* of the sacrament. There is also a material element, the ablution of water, which is called the *matter* of the sacrament.

Institution by Jesus Christ. In these times of theological confusion, it is good to recall that the seven sacraments of the new law — Baptism, Confirmation, Eucharist, Penance, Anointing of the Sick, Holy Orders, and Matrimony — were all instituted by Jesus Christ our Lord (*Catechism of the Catholic Church*, Nos. 1114 and 1210).

Making present the grace it signifies. The sacraments are not to be seen as symbols which serve only to give evidence of the action

11

of God in the soul. They are the very **cause** of that grace, *ex opere operato*, "by virtue of the accomplished rite" (Ibid., p. 230). Saint Augustine explains this in a colourful way: "The water touches the heart while it cleanses the body." The grace that a sacrament produces is therefore very closely related to its material element: the water of the baptism causes the purification, the bread and the wine of the Eucharist evoke the food, etc... The *form* then serves to define the meaning of the material element: the words pronounced by the priest at baptism show that it consists of a *spiritual* purification, etc...

What are sacramentals?

The sacramentals are also known to be perceptible signs of grace. However, they differ from the sacraments, in the sense that they have not all been instituted by our Lord. Nor do they cause the grace *ex opere operato*, but rather *ex opere operantis Ecclesiae;* this means that they derive their effectiveness from the prayers of the Church. Among the sacramentals, we usually take into account certain prayers (the Our Father, the Confiteor...), the blessings, the sign of the cross, incense, holy water, etc...

What connection is there between the sacraments (and the sacramentals) and the liturgy?

The essential connection is this: the rites which are used in the administration of the sacraments are entirely liturgical rites. One could just as well say that the liturgy itself is a great sacrament.

Here lies the fundamental importance of the signs in the liturgy: while resolutely turning its back on Manicheism (according to which the material universe is intrinsically evil, doomed to sin by nature) as well as on Protestantism (for which the material order of things is powerless to convey grace), the Church attaches primary importance to the material world in the work of the Redemption. Whether it be the flame of the candle, the smoke of incense, the fragrance of the chrism, or the sacred vestment of the priest, these are all components which make the liturgy what it is.

II

SACRAMENT AND SACRIFICE

At the heart of the sacramental body of the Church, whence the grace of our sanctification is drawn, there stands out a sacrament so eminent in comparison to the others that it is called the Holy or Blessed Sacrament. This is the Eucharist. Different from the other sacraments which only confer grace, the Eucharist contains the Author of grace Himself.

What is the sacrament of the Eucharist?
The Catechism of Saint Pius X gives us the following definition:

"The Eucharist is a sacrament in which, by the marvellous conversion of the whole substance of bread into the Body of Jesus Christ, and that of wine into His precious Blood, is contained truly, really, and substantially, the Body, Blood, Soul and Divinity of the same Lord Jesus Christ, under the appearance of bread and wine as our spiritual food."

For what reasons did our Lord institute the Eucharist?
First of all, it was to serve as spiritual food for our souls. Saint Thomas explains this in a concise formula: *consecratur ut sumatur*, (this sacrament) is consecrated in order to be eaten. Secondly, it was so that the Church would have a sacrifice capable of conferring on us the merits of Jesus Christ by which we have been redeemed. The paschal lamb, which the Hebrews offered in the Old Testament, and its flesh of which they then took communion, was a prefiguration of this sacrament.

Why is it said that the Eucharist is also a sacrifice?
We have seen that the proper feature of the sacrament is to achieve what it signifies. In the case of the Eucharist, the presence throughout the Mass of the Body of our Lord, under

the species of bread, on the one hand, and then the presence of His Blood as though collected in the chalice, on the other, both precisely signify His Sacrifice on the Cross. At Mass, Christ offers Himself to His Father through the hands of the priest, thus perpetuating the precise act which was accomplished once and for all on Calvary. The Sacrifice of the Cross, made sacramentally present on our altars, is what we call *the Holy Sacrifice of the Mass*: "For as often as the memorial of this Victim is celebrated, the work of our Redemption is wrought" (Secret of the 9th Sunday after Pentecost).

To what ends do we offer a sacrifice to God?

1. In order to give Him the honour which is owed Him. It is a *latreutical* sacrifice (from the Greek *latreia,* which signifies the service owed to a master).

2. In order to thank Him for His good deeds. It is a *eucharistical* sacrifice (the Greek word *eucharistia* means the action of giving thanks).

3. In order to appease Him by the offering of reparation for our sins. It is a *propitiatory* sacrifice (its goal is to render us favorable before God).

4. In order to obtain the graces which are necessary to us. It is an *impetratory* sacrifice (from the Latin *impetrare,* 'to ask').

What are the fruits of the Mass?

They are the graces which this Sacrifice will confer upon souls. Usually, we distinguish them as follows:

1. The *general* fruit. The whole Church, including all of the faithful, take part in the fruit of each celebrated Mass: the living, as well as the dead, as it is stated in the prayers of the Canon.

2. The *special* fruit applies to those for whom the Mass is specially offered. This usually corresponds to the intention for which the celebrant priest has received a *Mass honorarium* [Mass stipend]; but it can also apply to any particular intention which he might want to add to the first.

3. Finally, the *personal* fruit is profitable both to the priest and all those assisting, for this is what is prayed for at the Offertory

of the bread: "...this spotless host, which I, Thy unworthy servant, offer unto Thee, my living and true God, for my innumerable sins, offenses, and negligences, and for all here present..."

Finally, we join the Catechism of the Council of Trent in saying that there exists a very close link between the doctrine of the Mass, which is the true Sacrifice of the new covenant, and the liturgical rites which accompany its celebration: "The Sacrifice (of the Mass) is celebrated with many solemn rites and ceremonies... All of them tend to display the majesty of this august Sacrifice, and to excite the faithful when beholding these saving mysteries, to contemplate the divine things which lie concealed in the Eucharistic Sacrifice."

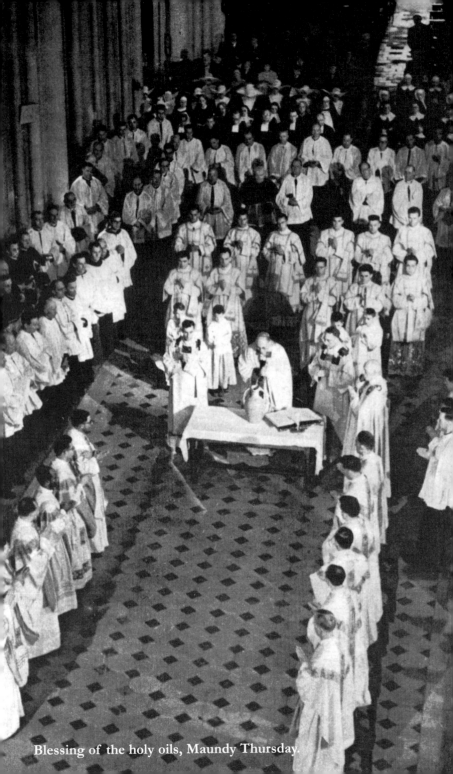

Blessing of the holy oils, Maundy Thursday.

III

The Liturgy

Where does the word "liturgy" originate?

The Greek word *leitourgia* has its roots in *leitos*, which means public, and *ergon*, an action or function. In ancient Athens, it indicated a public office carried out in view of the common good: for example, the equipping of a war ship, or even the financing of a great theatrical production. Early in the Christian tradition this word was used to describe the Mass, and later the whole of the sacred functions.

How do we define Christian liturgy?

At the beginning of our "discovery," we read that the celebration or the administration of a sacrament was entirely a liturgical act; therefore it can be looked upon as a great sacramental. This doctrine was developed by Pius XII in the encyclical *Mediator Dei* (November 20, 1947) and summarized in paragraph 7 of *Sacrosanctum Concilium* (December 4, 1963): "The liturgy, then, is rightly seen as an exercise of the priestly office of Jesus Christ. It involves the presentation of man's sanctification under the guise of signs perceptible by the senses and its accomplishment in ways appropriate to each of these signs. In it full public worship is performed by the Mystical Body of Jesus Christ, that is, by the Head and His members."

Therefore, there are two movements in the liturgy: one descending, that is Christ sanctifying men; and another ascending, that is Christ rendering to His Father the worship of which He is worthy. A worship which only He, the perfect Priest, can render, and one in which He associates all the faithful, who are the members of His mystical Body.

What exactly does "public" worship signify?

There are three degrees which can be considered in the

worship which man renders to God. First of all, there is individual prayer: "But thou, when thou shalt pray, enter into thy chamber, and having shut the door, pray to thy Father in secret: and thy Father, who seeth in secret, will reward thee" (Matt. 6:6). But man is a social being: even though there exists private practice, there is no such thing as individual religion. This is why our Lord also calls for collective prayer: "Again I say to you, that if two of you shall agree upon earth, concerning any thing whatsoever they shall ask, it shall be done to them by my Father, who is in heaven. For where there are two or three gathered together in my name, there am I in the midst of them" (Matt. 18:19-20).

This collective worship, however, is not always a public one because the public worship is actually the prayer of Christ and His Church. In other words, it is the official prayer of the Church, which is celebrated in her name by her ministers, those whom she has ordained to do so: namely priests, deacons, religious, etc.

As examples, let us take two extremes. A hermit, isolated in his oratory in the mountains, celebrates Mass or recites the Office of Vespers: this is a public prayer, because it is liturgical. On the other hand, a crowd of thousands sings the *Ave Maria* in front of the grotto of Lourdes: this is considered private prayer. However, this same crowd attending Mass afterwards will participate in public prayer. The Church has always recognized a particular efficacy on the part of public worship: "For if the prayer of one or two possesses such power, how much more that of the bishop and the whole Church!" (Saint Ignatius of Antioch, *Letter to the Ephesians,* V).

If we really want to grasp the secret of the liturgy, then we must first of all see in it a song from Heaven. In fact, from all eternity, the Holy Trinity is like the Temple of a grandiose liturgy: God sings, Himself to Himself, within the secret of His life, an eternal hymn which is nothing but the very expression of His perfections within His Word and His Spirit. To this song, as seen in the Apocalypse, are united the angels and the saints in heaven. And man? Excluded from this concert by the sin of our first parents, it will not be long before he is readmitted: "By assuming human nature, the Divine Word introduced into this earthly exile a hymn which is sung in heaven for all eternity" (*Mediator Dei*, 144).

The liturgy and the liturgies.

As when the sun shines through a prism there is a spectrum of various colours, so then, as this unique celestial canticle travels through the infirmity of this present life, it finds itself divided into various melodies: the Christian liturgy, having been born simultaneously in different parts of the world, has adopted different modes of expression. From these, we notice very early on that there were two great liturgical groups: the Western, Latin tradition, and the Eastern.

In the West, there stands first of all the Roman Rite, from which the Church of Rome, "Mother and Teacher of all Churches", spread to a point where it almost totally supplanted the other Latin rites. Its prime characteristic is that of beautiful **sober** ceremonies, **concise** prayers, and great **dogmatic precision**, all in a neat literary form rythmed by the *cursus* of the Latin sentence structure. In it, the Church is the worthy heir of nearly eight centuries of Greco-Latin civilization.

The Following surviving rites are closely related to the Roman Rite: the Lyonese, the Milanese (or Ambrosian), the Dominican, and the Carthusian. However, Gaul had known from the first centuries a Latin liturgy which differs greatly from the Roman Rite: the Gallican liturgy was undoubtedly influenced by the Eastern liturgies, from which it derived an often exuberant lyricism. By order of Charlemagne in the eighth century, it was gradually replaced by the Roman Rite, which did not hesitate to borrow many of its splendid texts and ceremonies.

Related to this Gallican Rite, the Mozarabic (or Visigothic) Rite, which was used in Spain, has also suffered a similar fate: various popes imposed the Roman Rite in Spain in order to reinforce the unity of the Church. An exception, however, was made in Toledo, where by a special privilege it has been conserved until the twentieth century; a reformed version is now permitted throughout Spain.

19

In the East, the various rites form two great families: the Syrian, and the Alexandrian. In the former group we find the Assyro-Chaldean Rite, the Syro-Malabar Rite, the Jacobite Rite, the Maronite Rite, the Byzantine Rite, and the Armenian Rite. In the second group there are the Coptic and the Egyptian Rites. But among all these, it is the Byzantine Rite which has become the most widespread: the liturgies of Saint John Chrysostom and of Saint Basil, which have been adopted by all the churches of the Orthodox communion.

This is not to say that all the faithful of the Byzantine Rite are "Orthodox," and therefore separated from Rome. The questions of rite and ecclesial communion are separate and distinct: the Byzantine liturgy may be celebrated by the Orthodox dissidents, but it is also celebrated by churches united to Rome, such as the Melkites, the Ruthenians, and others. Inversely, the Roman Mass is also celebrated by certain schismatics such as the Old Catholics, the Latin Church of Toulouse, and others. Sometimes it is even done invalidly: for example, by Anglican ministers who have not been validly ordained.

Diversity or unity?

Is such a variety of rites compatible with the unity of the Church? The popes have never ceased to affirm it: "As all are aware, that [unity] does not prevent the use and approval in the Catholic Church of various rites, by which she is displayed in greater beauty and, like the daughter of the King of Kings, seems to be dressed in varied robes" (John XXIII, *Ad Petri Cathedram*, June 29, 1959). This does not mean that one should do whatever he pleases, but rather, that the rites of antiquity will be faithfully guarded: "The noble and glorious antiquity of the various rites is the ornament of the whole Church... Perhaps nothing illustrates better the note of Catholicity in the Church of God than the singular homage of the different forms of these ceremonies, celebrated in languages venerable in their antiquity, and made all the more sacred by the use which the Apostles and the Fathers made of them. That homage is, as it were, a renewal of the exceptional homage rendered to Christ, the Divine Founder of the Church, by the Wise Men who came from the different parts of the East 'to adore Him'" (Leo XIII, *Orientalium Dignitatis,* November 30, 1894).

What is the principal quality of the liturgy?

Without doubt, it is the sense of the sacred. It is the liturgy's proper duty to express the transcendence of God; it must, with the fewest possible imperfections, reflect the holiness of angelical choirs . As the official prayer of the Mystical Body of Jesus Christ, it must therefore avoid getting caught up in the vulgar and the arbitrary, as is so often the case today: "The liturgy has become for many a structuring exercise where groups make up their own 'liturgies' from one week to the next with a zeal that is often as admirable as it misplaced. This profound rupture of the liturgical conscience seems to me to be the most fatal thing there is. The boundaries which separate liturgy and student meetings are gradually disappearing..." (Cardinal Ratzinger, *Communio,* Nov. 1977, p. 42). The *Catechism of the Catholic Church* also states that "no sacramental rite may be modified or manipulated at the will of the minister or the community. Even the supreme authority in the Church may not change the liturgy arbitrarily, but only in the obedience of faith and with religious respect for the mystery of the liturgy" (# 1125).

The Supper at Emmaus (Rembrandt)

IV

FROM THE BEGINNING

It is spring of the year 55. Saint Paul is writing to the Corinthians: "For I have received of the Lord that which also I delivered to you, that the Lord Jesus, the night in which he was betrayed, took bread and giving thanks broke it, and said: *Take ye, and eat: this is my body, which shall be delivered for you: do this for the commemoration of me.* In like manner also the chalice, after he had supped, saying: *This chalice is the new testament in my blood: this do ye, as often as you shall drink it for the commemoration of me.*" This is the most ancient account of the institution of the Eucharist to have been handed down to us. Still today, it remains at the heart of each Mass.

Less than a century later, we find Justin writing to the pagan emperor Antoninus Pius (138-161), explaining what Christians did: "On the day we call the day of the sun, all who dwell in the city or country gather in the same place. The memoirs of the apostles and the writings of the prophets are read, as much as time permits. When the reader has finished, he who presides over the gathering admonishes and challenges them to imitate these beautiful things. Then we all rise together and offer prayers for ourselves... and for all others, wherever they may be, so that we may be found righteous by our life and actions, and faithful to the commandments, so as to obtain eternal salvation. When the prayers are concluded we exchange the kiss. Then someone brings bread and a cup of water and wine mixed together to him who presides over the brethren. He takes them and offers praise and glory to the Father of the universe, through the name of the Son and of the Holy Spirit and for a considerable time he gives thanks (in Greek: *eucharistian*) that we have been judged worthy of these gifts. When he has concluded the prayers and thanksgiving, all present give voice to an acclamation by saying: *Amen.* When he

Byzantine worship.

who presides has given thanks and the people have responded, those whom we call deacons give to those present the "eucharisted" bread, wine and water and take them to those who are absent."

Here the order of our Mass is easily recognized; however, the Roman liturgy has not yet attained its full development. We notice the absence of the entrance rites (the Introit and Kyrie will be introduced a few centuries later), and the Mass begins right away with the readings: the little domestic churches are without the *ampleur* of the sumptuous basilicas which were built following the Peace of the Church (313, the emperor Constantine's edict of Milan) and which will naturally also have called for a grandiose liturgical deployment. We notice as well with Saint Justin, that the Eucharistic Prayer is still not yet following a strict standard formula: a certain amount of improvisation is left to the celebrant, a point which today is no longer relevant. Without having any relation whatsoever with the numerous aberrations of our day and age, the improvisation under the Old Testament, and later in the primitive Church, would obey very precise rules: the themes of "thanksgivings" flowed according to a dynamic stereotyped model; and the faithful would recognize in the text a number of key expressions.

Let us leap ahead four centuries to the time of Saint Gregory the Great (Pope, 590-604). The general order of the texts and ceremonies of the Roman Mass is already very close to the one we know today: the procession of ministers makes its way toward the sanctuary while the Introit is being sung. Having arrived before the altar, the celebrant silently prays for a few moments (this is the origin of the prayers at the foot of the altar). The other ceremonies follow: Kyrie, Gloria, Collect sung by the celebrant, Epistle read by a subdeacon, Gradual and Alleluia carried out by the cantors, and Gospel proclaimed by a deacon, escorted by torches and heard by everyone standing. Then there are the ceremonies of the Offertory which, at the time, mostly consisted of the reception of the offerings (which has survived until today in the form of the collection), the Secret, the Preface, the Canon (with very little variation from what is found today in our traditional Missal), the Pater Noster, the Communion, etc.

Throughout the Middle Ages, the liturgy of the Mass will continue to be developed and enriched. Various prayers appear: at the foot of the altar, during the Offertory, before and after the Communion of the Priest. Many gestures will be added - genuflections, signs of the cross, inclinations - which for a gathering of people sensitive to signs will emphasize the sacred and the sacrificial aspects of the Mass. But after this harmonious period of liturgical developments, about two centuries of decadence followed, and so the Council of Trent demanded a return to the "ancient norms of the holy Fathers." Saint Pius V was responsible for this revision and imposed the Missal of the Roman Court on the whole of the Roman Church, except for those liturgies already in existence for over two centuries. This missal, which had remained faithful to the ancient Roman Rite, was then to become known as the "Missal of Saint Pius V."

Vézelay

The Pope surrounded by his deacons.

V

From High to Low Mass

We have so far presented a brief history of the Mass throughout the ages in its solemn celebration and in the presence of the faithful and the ministers. It is within this setting that the liturgy was developed. The Introit, the Kyrie, and the Gradual were not texts to be read by the celebrant, but were chants rendered by the schola or the assembly. The celebrant's function is quite different: as mediator between God and men, he prays in the name of everyone and offers the sacrifice. The function of the deacon is distinct: he proclaims the Gospel and assists the celebrant at the altar. So is the function of the lectors, who proclaim the Word of God in the Epistle or Prophecy; so is the function of the cantors and the acolytes. In order to understand the rites of the Mass, it is most important to keep these distinctions in mind. Today still, in its solemn pontifical celebration, the liturgy, which is an epiphany of the Church, truly is a great manifestation which gathers around the bishop, the priests[1], the deacons, subdeacons, and the other ministers, amid the great flock of the people. It is then that it reflects most perfectly the celestial liturgy, which is shown us in the Apocalypse with its procession of elders and of angels, with the multitude of the chosen ones, all grouped around the Altar and the Throne of the Lamb, in the midst of the clouds of incense and the most sublime chants.

But the splendor of the pontifical liturgy is not readily available to all. What will be, then, the fate of those parishes which are not favoured with a great number of clerics, or those lesser populated monasteries? It is within this context that the high Mass will appear, or as it is often said, the Mass "with deacon and subdeacon", a sort of reduction of the grand

---

1 The Pontifical Mass, celebrated by the bishop in his cathedral, always takes into account the canons who, though clothed in sacred vestments, do not concelebrate as such.

function of the pontifical, which was more adapted to small gatherings. Two other degrees of lesser solemnity will also rapidly make their appearance in history: the sung Mass, in which the celebrant takes on, in addition to his own role, that of the deacon (singing the Gospel, putting the wine in the chalice, dismissing the congregation with the chanting of the *Ite missa est*) and that of the subdeacon (reading of the Epistle, purification and cleansing of the chalice). And finally, there is the low Mass in which the celebrant will, in a manner of speaking, exercise concurrently all the above functions: in addition to the roles of the deacon and the subdeacon; he will also be cantor and recite the parts which were ordinarily sung (Introit, Gradual, Alleluia, Offertory, etc.). For this reason, many of the low Mass ceremonies will find their explanation in the solemn or pontifical Masses. Low Mass is, in a way, their reduced format. Therefore, our explanation will follow the course of the solemn liturgy, while taking care to identify when needed the simplified rites of low Mass.

Why fixed and stable rites?

This stability is essential to the notion of sacredness in itself. The liturgy ought to express the transcendence of God. It must reflect, in the most perfect way, the holiness of the angelic choirs. As the official prayer of the mystical Body of Jesus Christ, it must avoid domination by the ordinary and the arbitrary, as is too often the case today: "The liturgy has become for many a structuring exercise where groups make up their own 'liturgies' from one week to the other with a zeal that is often as admirable as it misplaced. This profound rupture of the liturgical conscience seems to me to be the most fatal thing there is. The boundaries which separate liturgy and student reunions are imperceptibly disappearing..." (Cardinal Ratzinger, *Communio,* Nov. 1977, p.42). In itself, ritualized actions prevent liturgical gatherings from adapting what is supposed to happen into something corresponding to their own subjective ideals and desires.

VI

Let us Enter Within the Church

A Christian church is normally directed towards the East. Throughout the Mass the faithful, as well as the celebrant at the altar, are all turned towards the rising sun. The symbolism here is very rich.

Firstly, the earthly paradise is traditionally thought to have been in the East: "The Christian churches are turned toward the East, in order that our gaze may be directed toward the paradise, our ancient fatherland, from which we have been chased away. And we pray Our Lord to re-entrust to us this place from which we were chased away" (Pseudo-Athanasius).

Secondly, in agreement with Holy Scripture, the Fathers see the image of the glorious Christ in the rising sun: "It is from the East, says Origen, that comes salvation; from there comes that man called Orient, mediator between God and men" (*Homel. IX in Lev. n. 10*). The rising sun is also an image of the Risen Christ "for that sun which seems to be dying in the West, we see it rise again with such glory in the East" (Honorius of Autun), and about the *Parousia*, which is His return at the end of time: "The Lord Himself says to us: 'In the same way as lightning travels from the East to the West, so will it be for the coming of the Lord'; and it is for the very fact that we await His coming that we pray in the direction of the East" (Saint John Damascene). This last idea might not be very evocative for our contemporaries. However, is not the return of Christ in glory the very object of our hope? "For as long as you eat this bread and drink this cup, you proclaim the Lord's death until he comes" (I Cor. 11:26).

The different parts of the church.

The church usually consists of a *nave*, where the faithful are; one or more steps giving access to the *choir*, where the clergy stands (canons, religious, etc.), then to the *sanctuary*, the sacred space around the altar, whence the celebrant officiates with his ministers. (Where there are few clergy, e.g., as in a parochial church, the choir and the sanctuary are generally merged.)

The presence of steps ascending to the choir, then the sanctuary, and finally to the altar, does indicate an idea of transcendence. In order to meet with God, one must elevate oneself, detach oneself from earthly things: it was at the peak of Mount Sinai that Moses received the Law; it was from the top of a mountain that our Lord preached the Beatitudes, manifested His Glory to His disciples on the day of the Transfiguration, and consumed His sacrifice. This symbolism is illuminated by Psalm 42, which the celebrant recites before going up to the altar at the beginning of the Mass: "Oh send forth thy light and thy truth; let them lead me, let them bring me to thy holy hill and to thy dwelling."

At the centre of the sanctuary: the altar.

The altar, on which the priest will offer the Sacrifice, is not a simple table; it represents Jesus Christ: "The altar of the Holy Church, it is Christ Himself", declares the pontiff during the ordination of the subdeacon. Also, from antiquity the altar has been made of stone, which by its solidity, its weight, its resistance, is a sign of strength (in the Psalms, God is often called *my rock*); and, as Saint Peter declares before the Sanhedrin: "This is the stone which was rejected by you the builders, but which has become the head of the corner" (Acts 4:11). The altar is also anointed with Holy Chrism on the day of its dedication (*Christ* signifies *anointed*), then five crosses are engraved onto it, which symbolize the five wounds of Christ. Finally, it is covered with white linen cloths, which are an evocation of the glory of Christ, and adorned with seven candle holders for the solemn Mass of the bishop, in the same way Saint John had seen, in the Apocalypse, the Son of Man, Jesus Christ, surrounded by seven golden candle holders. A crucifix is placed on the altar, which recalls to mind the identity between the Sacrifice of the Mass and that of Calvary.

Why are relics placed in the altar?

This is a practice that stems from a pagan custom, from the ancient Roman religion: on the anniversary day of the death of a relative, the family would gather around the grave in order to share a ritual meal there. In the same way, the first Christians came to celebrate the anniversary of martyrs by offering on their graves the Holy Sacrifice of the Mass (which Saint Thomas Aquinas calls the Sacred Banquet, *Sacrum Convivium*). With Constantine's edict of 313 the persecutions came to an end, and the Christian people could build great basilicas in honour of their martyrs, the inauguration of which gave way to great solemnities: amid a whole people overwhelmed with joy, the holy remains were transferred while Psalms were chanted, and were laid down under the altar of the Holy Sacrifice. Are not the martyrs, in the Christian view, sacred members of Christ, the immolated Victim on the altar?

Are there any illustrations of the altar in the Old Testament?

In the book of Genesis, the altar quickly appears as a privileged place to meet with God, first and foremost by the sacrifice which is offered upon it. Having just been saved from the waters and departed from the ark, Noah "built an altar to the Lord, and took of every clean animal and of every clean bird, and offered burnt offerings on the altar" (Gen. 8:20). An altar can also be raised up in order to remember a divine manifestation: "Abram passed through the land to the place at She'chem, to the oak of Mo'reh. Then the Lord appeared to Abram, and said, 'To your descendants I will give this land.' So he built there an altar to the Lord, who had appeared to him" (Gen. 12:6-7). In this case, the altar represents the place where God has visited his servant; it then becomes an opening into Heaven. Again, while consecrating with an anointing of oil the stone on which he had laid his head during the night when God appeared to him, Jacob cried out: "How awesome is this place! This is none other than the house of God, and this is the gate of heaven" (Gen. 28:17).

The Holy of Holies: the Tabernacle.

The little cabinet in which the consecrated Hosts are enclosed is usually placed on the main altar, a place of honour. However, in churches where some clerics are bound to choral recitation of the Holy Office (cathedrals, collegiate or abbatial churches), the tabernacle is traditionally found on another altar. On entering the church, the faithful genuflect before the tabernacle. If, however, the Blessed Sacrament is not kept here, a genuflection is still made in recognition of its eminent dignity, and of the altar cross which is mounted upon it. Usually, clergy members follow these same rules, except for the celebrant priest, the prelates, the canons, and the monks who will make a profound inclination towards the altar when the Blessed Sacrament is not present.

VII

The Celebrant and His Ministers

Who is it that offers to God the Holy Sacrifice of the Mass?

The *Catechism of Saint Pius X* answers: "The first and principal Offeror of the Holy Sacrifice of the Mass is Jesus Christ, while the priest is the minister who in the name of Jesus Christ offers the same Sacrifice to the Eternal Father." Whence the expression *Sacerdos alter Christus,* the priest is another Christ. Let us then put aside right away those modern theories which claim that the celebrant is only a delegate of the community, and would thence hold from this delegation the mission to "celebrate the Eucharist," independently of any sacramentally received ordination conferred by the bishop. Let us rather affirm with the *Catechism of the Catholic Church* that: "Only validly ordained priests can preside at the Eucharist and consecrate the bread and the wine so that they become the Body and Blood of the Lord" (1411).

Are the priests expected to celebrate the Mass every day?

The Church answers very clearly: "Remembering always that in the mystery of the Eucharistic Sacrifice the work of redemption is continually being carried out, priests are to celebrate frequently. Indeed, *daily celebration is earnestly recommended,* because, even if it should not be possible to have the faithful present, it is an action of Christ and of the Church in which priests fulfil *their principal role" (Canon 904).*

What about Masses without the faithful?

But does it make sense to have the Mass celebrated like this, by a priest in the absence of the faithful? Yes, it does, because "the Eucharist, even if the faithful cannot be present, is an act of Christ and of the Church, and deserves, by that very fact, to be celebrated in itself, because the reasons for offering the sacrifice are not to be understood only from the standpoint of the faithful to whom the sacraments must be administered, but mostly from the standpoint of God, to Whom a sacrifice is offered in the consecration of the sacrament."

How is the celebrant assisted in the celebration of the Mass?

As the nine choirs of angels celebrate the celestial liturgy around the throne of God in the same manner in which they silently assisted our Lord in the offering of His Sacrifice on Calvary, the ministers of the altar also assist the priest in the celebration of the liturgy here on earth. The seven Spirits, who in St. John's Apocalypse stand day and night before the Throne of God, correspond to the seven *deacons* who were ordained by the Apostles. Instituted as early as the beginning of the third century to assist the deacons, the *subdeacons*, like the deacons, are equally looked upon, from the ninth century on, as sacred ministers. The inferior ministers who have roles (derived from that of the subdeacon) to play in the Mass are the *acolyte* and the *lector*. There also exist other functions within the Mass: the *thurifer* (bearer of the censer) and the *torch bearers* (who bear the lit torches during the Consecration), but these are only subdivisions of the ministry of acolyte.

What are the vestments of the ministers of the altar?

The traditional common liturgical vestment of all clerics is the white *alb*, a long tunic reaching almost to the floor. Among the secular clergy, the inferior ministers often wear the *surplice*, a diminutive of the alb, over the *soutane* (cassock). Before the alb, the *amice*, a white linen veil, is put on, which among religious is worn like a hood, but among the secular clergy is simply worn around the neck. The alb is secured at the waist by the *cincture*: in the Book of Exodus, God commands Moses to eat the Paschal meal "with a girdle around your waist," a precaution designed to facilitate walking, and which symbolizes by that very fact the ready disposition to serve God, and the detachment of earthly goods.

The sacred ministers (priest, deacon, and subdeacon) wear a small band of cloth on the left arm: the *maniple*, which in

Roman antiquity was a sign of dignity. In addition, the priest and the deacon put on the *stole*, a long band of material worn crossed on the chest by the priest and like a banner on the left shoulder by the deacon. This represents the priestly power: therefore the priest wears it for the administration of all the sacraments. Finally, the deacon puts on the *dalmatic*, and the subdeacon puts on the *tunicle*. This presentation is the proper order of the vestments. As for the priest, when he celebrates Mass he puts on the *chasuble*, a large vestment worn over the other vestments. It has an opening just for the head, and is then harmoniously draped upon the arms. Throughout the centuries, this vestment was shortened and opened on the sides, and finally came to be in later years what was called the "fiddle-back." Under the influence of Dom Guéranger, a French reformer of the Roman liturgy in the last century, the chasuble has reemerged in its traditional ample form.

When celebrating a solemn Mass the bishop also adds, over the regular priestly vestments, the *tunicle and dalmatic*, which evoke the plenitude of the priestly power. He also wears the *mitre*, the *sandals* (a kind of embroidered shoes), the *gloves,* and lastly the *ring,* which symbolizes his union with the Church and his diocese. He bears in hand the *crosier*, or pastoral staff, which is a sign of the mission he has received to tend the flock of our Lord.

Papal procession at
St Peter's, Rome

THE ENTRANCE RITES

Introibo ad altare Dei, ad Deum
qui laetificat juventuten meam.
Prayers at the foot of the altar

VIII

The Entrance Rites

The Aspersion.

On entering the church to attend Mass, the faithful sign themselves with holy water. On Sunday, however, the individual signing of oneself is replaced by a collective aspersion, which the celebrant does before beginning the high Mass. Let us see what this rite signifies.

In the same way that the baptismal waters opened the doors of the Church for us and then those of the Kingdom of Heaven, holy water also refreshes baptismal grace within us, purifies us anew, and then introduces us into the church for the celebration of the Holy Mysteries. The blessing of the water and the public aspersion occur every Sunday, the day of the Resurrection of our Lord, in order to recall the blessing of the baptismal waters which occurs every year during the night of Easter. It is therefore a rite which bears a profound spiritual significance.

The procession.

The Mass itself begins with the Entrance Procession. At the high Mass of a feast day, the solemn procession consists of the celebrant preceded by the deacon, the subdeacon, the master of ceremonies, the torch bearers, the acolytes, and the thurifer. At a low Mass, the simple procession consists only of the celebrant and his server. This procession bears a great significance: the celebrant and his ministers who make their way towards the sanctuary and the altar represent the Church of the earth, the Church militant walking towards the celestial city, under the leadership of Jesus Christ. At the head of the Entrance Procession are carried the censer and the candlesticks, a privilege which in pagan antiquity was enjoyed by the emperor and high Roman dignitaries. On certain occasions (monastic rites, pontifical Masses, etc.), the book of the Gospels is also carried in a way similar to the Roman magistrates who used to be preceded by the code, the *liber mandatorum*. Are not the Gospels the Law *par excellence*, and the priest, an *alter Christus*? Is He not more than all the emperors? It is for this very reason that at a low Mass the servant must carry the Missal before the celebrant.

The Introit.

Such a majestic Entrance Procession calls for an appropriate musical accompaniment, an opening hymn, which introduces the faithful to a mood proper to the feast that is celebrated. This is the Introit, which is sung by the choir while the ministers make their way towards the altar. Ror example, there is the Introit of Christmas Night, which says in a very soft and recollecting melody: *Dominus dixit ad me* "The Lord hath said to me: Thou art my Son, this day I have begotten Thee." Or the ardent supplication of the Second Sunday in Lent: *Reminiscere,* "Remember, O Lord, Thy bowels of compassion, and Thy mercies that are from the beginning of the world, lest at any time our enemies rule over us!" Or again, the splendid *Signum magnum* of 15th August: "A great sign appeared in heaven: a woman clothed with the sun, and the moon under her feet, and on her head a crown of twelve stars?" With the generalization of the low Mass, the Introit is recited by the priest at the beginning of the Mass.

IX

AT THE FOOT OF THE ALTAR

Once the Entrance Procession is completed, the celebrant and his ministers recite the Prayers at the Foot of the Altar. In the first centuries, this was an extended period of silent prayer. The celebrant prostrated himself completely and prayed silently before the altar. This is the most expressive attitude of adoration, which the Roman liturgy still observes at the beginning of the liturgy of Good Friday. It is an attitude which is eminently biblical: "When Abram was ninety-nine years old the Lord appeared to him and said: I am God Almighty. Bear yourself blameless in my presence, and I will make a covenant between me and thee... Abram bowed to the ground..." (Gen. 17:1–2). This is an attitude of adoration which gives a profound feeling of humility: this God whom I adore is everything; therefore, I am but nothing before Him.

The Prayers at the Foot of the Altar were born out of this silent prayer. Their content has varied somewhat throughout the ages, depending on the area and the particular liturgies of dioceses or religious orders. In the Roman Rite, they generally consist of the *Confiteor*, where the celebrant expresses his unworthiness before ascending to the altar, preceded by the Psalm *Judica me,* which was chosen because of its fourth verse: "I will go in to the altar of God, to God who giveth joy to my youth." Therefore, the Prayers at the Foot of the Altar are by their very nature private prayers. At a sung Mass, the celebrant must say them in such a way that only his ministers can hear them, while the faithful join in the chanting of the *Introit,* the hymn that is sung in its place. At a low Mass, the celebrant will pronounce them in a louder fashion so that the faithful too might respond. This custom of the dialogue Mass has prevailed since the period following World War I [especially in continental Europe - Ed.]. Therefore, whenever the Propers are not being sung, the faithful rightfully respond to these prayers along with the servers.

Ascending to the altar, the celebrant then recites a prayer of great symbolic importance: "Take away from us our iniquities, we beseech Thee, O Lord, that we may be worthy to enter with pure minds into the Holy of Holies." The Christian altar is, in fact, the Holy of Holies of the New Covenant.

The kiss of the altar. We have seen that the altar is the central point, the heart of the church: "The altar of holy Church is Christ himself, as Saint John says in Apocalypse 8:3; he has seen a golden altar raised before the throne, on which and by which are consecrated the offerings of the faithful" (*Roman Pontifical,* Ordination of Subdeacons). As soon as he has arrived at the altar, the celebrant brings his lips to the sacred stone in order to express his veneration for Christ. Thus the custom has been, since the Middle Ages, to place pieces of martyrs' bones in the altar. The celebrant concludes the preparatory prayers in this way: "We beseech Thee, O Lord, by the merits of Thy Saints, whose relics are here, and of all the Saints, that Thou wouldst vouchsafe to forgive me all my sins. Amen."

In the Roman Rite, the celebrant omits the Prayers at the Foot of the Altar when the Mass immediately follows another liturgical function, such as the blessing of palms or ashes, or the Office of Terce in monasteries.

Incensation by the deacon (Byzantine Rite)

X

THE SMOKE OF INCENSE

After having kissed the altar, the celebrant envelopes it with a sweet-smelling cloud. The use of incense was already prescribed in the Old Testament, and it is particularly the preparatory incensing of the annual Expiation rite which best evokes that which occurs at the beginning of the Mass: "Then Aaron is to fill a censer with live coals from the altar that stands before the Lord, and to take two handfuls of finely ground aromatic incense. He is to take these through the veil and then to put the incense on the fire before the Lord, and with a cloud of incense he must cover the throne of mercy that is on the Testimony?" (Lev. 16:12–13). In the same way, while going around the altar, the celebrant "covers it with a cloud of incense."

What is the symbolism of incense?

Carried at the head of a procession and then wafted about the altar, the incense first brings to mind the idea of purification: the Church recognizes that it has the particular power of banishing evil spirits. Before burning the incense on the altar at the dedication of a church, the bishop blesses it using these words: "Bless and sanctify this incense, Thy creature, so that in smelling its perfume, all the languors, the infirmities, and the treacheries of the enemy, will flee from man, whom you have created and redeemed by the precious blood of your Son, in order that he may never be hurt by the bite of the serpent." Incense is also used to cense the candles of Candlemas, ashes, palms, and the offerings of the Mass.

Second, the incense symbolizes the prayer which rises towards God, as in this psalm verse which the priest recites at the censing of the Offertory: "May my prayers rise like incense, my hands like the evening offering" (Ps. 140).

Finally, incense is universally recognized as a form of adoration rendered to God; an adoration which is intimately linked to the idea of sacrifice: offering incense to idols during the time of antiquity constituted a sacrifice to the gods. And the Latin word *thus*, which signifies incense, takes its origins from the Greek verb *thuo*, which is sacrifice. At Mass, it is this act of adoration which brings about the censing of the Host at the Elevation, the cross at the altar, the book of the Gospels, and the priest who is *alter Christus*. For this same reason also, censing is done to relics of saints, and even to the faithful, who by their baptism have become members of Christ. Let us notice that one and the same rite of censing can have two significations: the censing of the faithful is both a purification and an honor rendered to Christ present within them.

Heaven.

Once more, incense brings to mind the celestial liturgy: "Another angel, who had a golden censer, came and stood at the altar. A large quantity of incense was given to him to offer with the prayers of all the saints on the golden altar that stood in front of the throne; and so from the angel's hand the smoke of the incense went up in the presence of God and with it the prayers of the saints. Then the angel took the censer and filled it with the fire from the altar, which he then threw down on to the earth." (Rev. 8: 3-5). What other symbol but that of this divine fire, taken from the celestial altar and thrown onto the earth, could have better expressed the relation which exists between our earthly liturgies and that of Heaven

XI

THE KYRIE AND GLORIA

After the Intoit, the choir intones the *Kyrie*. When it first appeared in the Roman Mass during the sixth century, this chant, somewhat like the response *ora pro nobis* of the litanies, was a response by the people to a series of long supplications chanted by a choir of cantors. The Roman liturgy, as well as many Eastern rites, has kept it in the original Greek. The vernacular "Lord have mercy," which is still too often imposed on the faithful, is gradually counting fewer and fewer adherents: "I admit that I prefer this prayer in the Greek, as it has been kept not only in the Eastern Church, but also in the Latin Church, right from the origins of Christianity" (Cardinal Lustiger, *La messe*, Bayard 1988, p.71).

Ever since Saint Gregory the Great, the Roman Mass has kept the number of three-times-three invocations, which expresses a Trinitarian supplication (the first three *Kyrie eleison* being addressed to the Father, the three *Christe* to the Son, and the last three *Kyrie* to the Holy Spirit). It also calls to mind the nine choirs of angels. On the other hand, the invocation of the *Kyrie eleison* has been justly considered as the summary of the whole prayer of the New Testament: it is the supplication of the blind man from Jericho and of the Canaanite woman, "Lord, Son of David, have mercy on me!"

On Sundays and on feast days, after the *Kyrie* the celebrant intones the *Gloria*. This hymn of joy and praise begins by proclaiming the message of the angels on Christmas eve, and again manifests the constant union of our liturgies with those of Heaven. It is sung every day in Paschaltide, and is omitted during the penitential seasons of Advent, Lent and during commemorations of the dead, etc.

During the *Kyrie* and the *Gloria* the faithful are standing. If kneeling is an exact expression of our nothingness before God, of our subjection and of our adoration, and rightly expected of us at the Consecration and Communion, the standing position is a no less important and fundamental liturgical attitude. It is such a natural position that very little attention is usually given to it. It serves mostly to instil a sense of respect: as it is proper to stand to greet a superior (the faithful stand while the celebrant processes in, for the priest is another Christ), so we also stand in His presence (as is done during the Gospel). However, it is also an attitude of prayer: the monks sing the Office while standing, and even earlier, in ancient Judaism "to stand" could simply mean "to pray."

In the Mass, the standing position also has another symbolism: as the Hebrews had to eat their first paschal lamb "with a girdle round the waist, sandals on their feet, staff in the hand" (Ex. 12:11) before heading towards the Promised Land, it is in this same manner that we celebrate the paschal sacrifice of the true Lamb of God. And Saint Iraneus, along with all the Church Fathers, has seen in standing "a symbol of the Resurrection by which, through the grace of Christ, we have been freed from sin and death."

Finally, it is the position in which the chosen ones celebrate the celestial liturgy: "After that I saw a countless number of people from every nation, race, tribe and language; they were standing in front of the throne and in front of the Lamb, dressed in white robes and holding palms in their hands. They shouted aloud, 'Victory to our God, who sits on the throne, and to the Lamb!'" (Rev. 7:9–10).

XII

The Collect

Both the supplication of the *Kyrie* and praise of the *Gloria* culminate in the prayer of petition: this is the Collect, which the celebrant recites in the name of the whole assembly. How could the union with God, the culmination of all liturgies, be the work of anyone but the priest, chosen from among the faithful and configured to Christ, to be their mediator before God?

The Collect is the first link of the Mass between the entrance rites it concludes and the office of readings it inaugurates. But, before this prayer, the celebrant once again kisses the altar, turns towards the faithful and greets them: *Dominus vobiscum!* In concise terms, this expression consists primarily of a wish: "The Lord be with you!" For this very reason the priest has just kissed the altar, so as to take Christ upon himself, whom he then in turn transmits to the assembly. Such a wish is frequently used in the Old Testament: "Now Boaz, as it happened, had just come from Bethlehem. 'The Lord be with you!' he said to the reapers. 'The Lord bless you!' they replied" (Ruth 2:4).

However, the *Dominus vobiscum* is more than a wish. Strictly speaking, it would have to be translated: "The Lord **is** with you", as Gideon was greeted by the angel: "The Lord with you, valiant warrior!" (Judges 6:12). It is thus the affirmation of a truth: "The Lord *is* with you." For assuredly, from the very beginning of the Mass, the Lord is already with the assembly; and this for two reasons: first, because each baptized person carries the living presence of the Lord in his soul; and second, because according to the promise of Jesus, "where two or three are gathered in my name, I am there in their midst." So we also translate *Dominus tecum* in the *Ave Maria*: "the Lord *is* with thee." To the bishop is reserved, in place of the *Dominus* *vobiscum*, the *Pax vobis*: "Peace with you." This is the sacerdotal greeting *par excellence*, the greeting of the risen Jesus to His apostles.

In saying *Dominus vobiscum*, the celebrant opens his arms in the direction of the assembly, as if to become one with them and to embrace them in the prayer which follows. The people respond *Et cum spiritu tuo*, "And with your spirit": a Hebrew way of saying "And with you too." It can be found in Saint Paul: "May the grace of the Lord Jesus Christ be with your spirit" (Phil. 4:23).

Then the celebrant invites the assembly to pray: *Oremus!* "Let us pray!", and recites the Collect (which is from the Latin *colligere*, which means 'to gather'). This prayer is the sum of the prayers of all the faithful that the celebrant gathers to present before God in his function of priest, mediator between God and men. During the Collect the celebrant stands, his arms extended towards heaven, a posture which he will also adopt for the other sacerdotal prayers: the Secret, the Postcommunion, the Preface, the Canon, and the *Pater*. It is the posture of the *orante*, common in Christian antiquity and so named because the Church is frequently represented in the catacomb paintings as a woman praying in this position. This posture is filled with profound human significance (the child reaching for the arms of his mother, the man who receives good news, or the soldier who surrenders). It is often in the Bible the stance of man before God, and it sometimes expresses praise: "All my life I will bless you, in your name I lift up my hands" (Ps. 62), or "Stretch out your hands towards the sanctuary, bless the Lord night after night!" (Ps. 133). Sometimes it expresses desire: "I stretch out my hands, like thirsty ground I yearn for you" (Ps.142); or the sacrificial offering: "My prayers rise like incense, my hands like the evening offering" (Ps. 140). It is thus a liturgical attitude present in the Old Testament: "And Solomon stood before the altar of the Lord, in the sight of the assembly of Israel, and spread forth his hands towards heaven, and said: Lord God of Israel, there is no God like thee, in heaven above, or on the earth." (III Kings 8:22). Finally, this attitude was inevitably

The 'Orante' posture, catacombe of Priscilla, Rome.

compared, from the very first centuries, to the position of Christ on the cross: the High-Priest of the new covenant in the offering of His sacrifice.

After having studied the ceremonies which pertain to the chant of the Collect, let us now look at the very text of these prayers. Let us also note that whatever is said in regard to the Collect also applies to the Secret (at the end of the Offertory) and the Postcommunion.

The form. Saint Thomas, in commenting on the Epistles of Saint Paul, teaches that the prayers of the Church consist of four parts (let us take, for example, the Collect of Easter Friday): 1. The elevation of the soul towards God (*oratio*):"Almighty and eternal God?" 2. Thanksgiving for a good which has been received (*gratiarum actio*): "In the Paschal mystery you instituted the covenant, whereby You forgave mankind." 3. The petition (*postulatio*): "Grant that what we outwardly celebrate we may follow in our deeds." 4. The conclusion (*obsecratio*); "Through our Lord Jesus Christ, Thy Son, who lives and reigns with Thee in the unity of the Holy Spirit, God for ever and ever." Throughout the whole liturgical year, with an infinite variety, the Church will follow this pattern.

The character of the Roman Collects. Born on Roman soil, our prayers have kept a particular flavour of the ancient Roman genius: simplicity and practical sense, sobriety and discipline, gravity and dignity. In their speech the Romans were to the point and abhorred verbiage. And so we have inherited from them this bedrock of substantial doctrine expressed with a rare precision in terminology, a logical cohesion of the different formulas, a literary beauty filled with sobriety, and finally, a thought so practical that it does not lie in words but instead aims right for the very acts: *res, non verba!* (The thing, not the word!)

The doctrine of the Collects. Father Emmanuel of Mesnil-Saint-Loup used to say that he had learned all about the theology of grace in the prayers of the Missal. Let us take a

The singing of the Collect at pontifical Mass.

look at the Collect of the Fourteenth Sunday after Pentecost: *Sine Te labitur humana mortalitas,* "without Thee the frailty of man is wont to fall" (original sin); *Tuis semper auxiliis ad salutaria dirigatur,* "save it [your Church]ever and lead it to all things profitable to salvation" (efficacious grace); and from the Sixteenth Sunday after Pentecost, *Tua nos, quaesumus Domine, gratia semper et proeveniat et sepuatur,* "May Thy grace, we beseech Thee, O Lord, ever go before us and follow us" (prevenient grace). Another example is the Collects of Lent, one for each day, which form a most beautiful treatise on Christian penance, etc.

The Collects of the feasts serve to reveal the heart of the mystery which is celebrated, its particular grace. At Epiphany we ask "that we, who know Thee now by faith, may be led on even to contemplate the beauty of Thy Majesty." On Palm Sunday, we ask "that we may deserve to possess not only the lessons of His patience, but also the fellowship of His Resurrection."

The response: Amen! This Hebrew word meaning 'firm' or 'solid', is used very often in the Bible (it is even the very last word of all the Holy Scriptures, for it closes the book of Revelation), as well as in the liturgy. It basically serves three purposes: 1. An affirmation. At the end of the *Credo,* for example, our *Amen* signifies "This is true, I affirm it." "To say *Amen* is to appose one's signature," says Saint Augustine. 2. A wish, the realization of which depends on God alone ("so be it"); for example, when we associate ourselves to the prayer of the priest for the repose of the soul of a faithful departed. 3. Our consent. When on the Saturday following Ash Wednesday, we ask that we might "faithfully observe the fast", our *Amen* means "Yes, I commit myself to that!" Let us note that in the heavenly liturgy, according to St. John in the Apocalypse, the *Amen* resounds without end. The life of the elect in heaven is a total adherence to God in an eternal *Amen.*

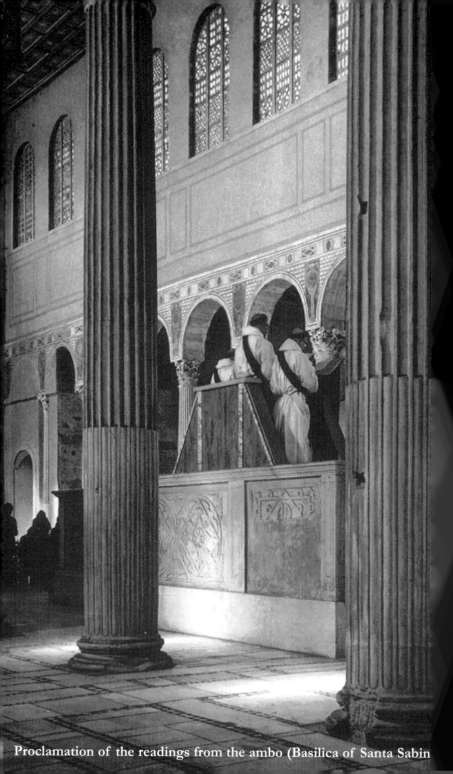

Proclamation of the readings from the ambo (Basilica of Santa Sabin

THE LITURGY OF THE WORD

Did not our hearts burn within us, when he talked
with us on the way and explained the Scriptures to us?
Gospel according to St Luke

XIII

THE READINGS

The reading of the sacred texts at Mass is a practice which goes back in time to the very origins of the Church: "On the day we call the day of the sun, all who dwell in the city or the country gather in the same place. The memoirs of the apostles and the writings of the prophets are read, as much as time permits. When the reader has finished, he who presides over those gathered admonishes and challenges them to imitate these beautiful things" (First *Apology* of Saint Justin, circa 150).

The second part of the Mass, commencing at the Offertory (the Liturgy of the Eucharist, or Mass of the Faithful, so named because the catechumens were then excluded), is centered on the altar and is, properly speaking, the Sacrifice. The first part (the Liturgy of the Word, or Mass of the Catechumens) is rather directed to the faithful: the readings are in fact meant for to their instruction. It is well to remark, however, that the Liturgy of the Word is not a preamble to the Mass, but rather it is verily part of the Sacrifice of the Eucharist: this God who will offer Himself in sacrifice, does He not bear the name of "The Word"? Is it not the same Lord, Saviour, and Redeemer who renders Himself spiritually present amidst us by the readings, and truly in His Sacrament? These are, says the *Imitation* (Book IV, Ch. 11), "the two tables set on either side in the storehouse of Thy holy Church. One is the table of the holy altar, having the holy Bread - that is, the precious Body of Christ; the other is that of the divine Law, containing holy doctrine, teaching the true faith, and leading most securely even beyond the veil of the Holy of Holies."

According to ancient usage the reader would stand at the limits of the sanctuary (which represents Heaven) and by the beginning of the nave (which represents the earth) on an elevated area (a sort of platform called the "ambo"), manifesting in this way that the Word of God descends from Heaven to earth, like a kind of pre-incarnation: "This is how you must understand the Scriptures," says Origen, "like the unique and perfect body of the Word." In the Roman Mass the number of readings has varied. In the Missal of Saint Pius V, there are generally two (Epistle and Gospel), sometimes three (for example, on Ember Wednesday), or even seven on Ember Saturdays, which is the survival of the long nocturnal vigil of ancient times, which would end towards daybreak on Sunday with the celebration of the glory of the Risen One.

At high Mass the Epistle is sung or read by the subdeacon, or, in his absence, by a reader, or even, if necessary, by the celebrant himself. Roman usage has been that the subdeacon proclaims the Epistle from the right side of the sanctuary, holding the book in his own hands. If it is the celebrant who is to read the Epistle, as is the case in a low Mass for example, he takes the same position (for he then exercises the role of subdeacon), standing on the right side of the altar, with his hands upon the book.

During this first reading, the faithful are seated: an attitude proper to a disciple, one who receives a teaching with docility; the attitude of Mary Magdalen sitting at the feet of Jesus, and by which she attracted the praise of the Master.

At the end of the Epistle, the faithful, or the server in their name, mark their assent with the acclamation: *Deo Gratias*! ("Thanks be to God!"). Then the subdeacon, in gratitude, goes and kisses the celebrant's hand, who in return blesses him silently.

Child musicians (Lucca Della Robbia)

XIV

THE GRADUAL, TRACT, AND ALLELUIA

In the Mass of the Catechumens, liturgists have recognized the three fundamentals of liturgical prayer: reading, praise, and prayer. "'In the reading,' says Dom Gréa, 'the Beloved (Christ) speaks to His Spouse (the Church), and He brings Her joy in the sound of His voice. In praise, the Spouse speaks of Her Beloved and delights in saying all of these beautiful things about Him. Finally, in the prayer, the Spouse, having found Her Beloved, then in turn speaks to Him, shares with Him Her desires, Her sorrows and Her joys, Her necessities and Her thanksgiving.'" (*La sainte liturgie*, p. 2). At Mass, the reading makes its way into our hearts, and evokes from them the echo of the chant.

After the Epistle comes the Gradual. Its name comes from the Latin *gradus*, "degree, or step of a staircase." This chant is so named because the soloist chanting it did not go up to the very top of the ambo, but remained on the stairs. The Gradual, like the Alleluia and the Tract, is very closely related to the liturgical time of the year or the particular mystery which is being celebrated. Its melody, which is quite ornate, and its long vocalization of syllables, makes it a very meditative chant. The text can either be followed in the Missal, or if the entire Proper of the Mass is sung, one can simply let oneself be carried by the melody.

The Gradual is usually followed by the Alleluia, which is destined to accompany the majestic procession which precedes the chanting of the Gospel, which will be discussed in the next chapter. "Alleluia" means "Praise God." According to the Book of Revelation (19:1-6), it is the triumphant chant of the chosen ones: "After this I seemed to hear the great sound of a huge crowd in heaven, singing: 'Alleluia. Victory and glory and power to our God.' Then the twenty-four elders and the four animals prostrated themselves and worshiped God seated there on His throne, and they cried, 'Amen, Alleluia.'"

The word "alleluia" is the object of long vocalizations on the vowel "a.". According to Saint Augustine, these express a praise which words simply cannot translate. At one time the cantors had to know the whole of the Gregorian repertoire by heart. In order to facilitate the learning of the long melismas, they set words to them. This is how the sequences were introduced (from the Latin *sequentia*, meaning "that which follows"), and they do 'follow' the Alleluia. There was an extraordinary proliferation of sequences in the Middle Ages of which Pope Saint Pius V kept only five: the *Victimae Paschali* of Easter, the *Veni Sancte Spiritus* of Pentecost, the *Lauda Sion* of Corpus Christi, the *Stabat Mater* of Our Lady of the Seven Sorrows, and the *Dies irae* of the Mass for the Dead.

In the Latin Church, the Alleluia is not heard during times of penance. At Mass, it is replaced by another meditative chant, the Tract. As shown by its name, it consists of a psalm which is sung as a whole, as a sort of long ornate psalmody (on some occasions, there are as many as ten verses).

After an absence of thirty days, the 'return of the Alleluia' during the Easter Vigil is, in cathedrals and abbeys, an event which is much celebrated. The subdeacon comes before the pontiff, who is sitting on his throne wearing the mitre, and declares to him: "Most Reverend Father, I hereby announce to you a great joy: it is the Alleluia!" The pontiff then doffs the mitre, and standing, he echoes in the silence the melody of the Paschal Alleluia, a bit hesitantly at the beginning, and finally in a triumphant manner.

XV

The Gospel

The proclamation of the Gospel, carried out with much solemnity, rightly appears as the culminating point of the Liturgy of the Word. First of all, only the deacon, or in his absence the celebrant, can perform this reading. He begins by kneeling at the foot of altar to pray that God might purify him, for it would be unthinkable for human lips to utter the Word of God without trembling: "Cleanse my heart and my lips, almighty God, who cleansed the lips of the prophet Isaias with a burning coal: through Thy gracious mercy be pleased so to cleanse me that I may proclaim Thy holy Gospel." Then the deacon takes the lectionary from the altar to signify that it is from Christ that the "Good News" comes to us. This is the true meaning of the Greek word *euangelion*. After this, the celebrant blesses him: "May the Lord be in your heart and on your lips that you may worthily and fitly proclaim His Gospel."

At this point, a procession takes place which involves all the ministers: as in the Entrance Procession the priest was preceded by the censor and the candles, so it is now the Gospel, held high by the deacon, which processes while receiving the honours of the light and the incense. Here the Gospel finds itself allotted the signs of adoration which are normally reserved for God: the deacon profoundly bows before it and censes it three times, as if it were the Blessed Sacrament. Our cathedrals have preserved some outstanding gold-inscribed lectionaries, made of crimson-dyed parchment, bound with ivory and studded with enamels and precious stones. These treasures are a true witness of times when the Faith was strong.

Before beginning the reading, every makes a sign of the cross three times: on the forehead, the lips, and the heart. This is to attune our senses and our being to the sacred text. During

The celebrant kisses the book of the Gospels.

the chanting of the Gospel, all stand, as would be done during the announcement of a joyful event, or as servants who await the commands of their master. The ancient customals teach us that the kings would remove their crowns; and, in Poland, the knights would grasp their swords, to show that they were ready to defend the Faith. The Old Testament gives us an example of this hastening to listen, while standing, to the Word of God: "And all the people were gathered together as one man, on the street which is before the water gate, and they spoke to Esdras, the scribe, to bring the book of the law of Moses, which the Lord had commanded to Israel. And Esdras opened the book before all the people: for he was above all the people: and when he had opened it, all the people stood. And Esdras blessed the Lord, the great God: and all the people answered: Amen, amen: lifting up their hands: and they bowed down, and adored God with their faces to the ground. And he read in the book of the law of God distinctly and plainly to be understood: and they understood when it was read" (Nehemiah 8).

At the end of the reading, the assembly gives assent by an acclamation. The most commonly used acclamation of the Middle Ages was *Amen*! as it is prescribed by Saint Benedict in his rule. According to the Missal of Saint Pius V, it would either be *Deo gratias* or *Laus tibi, Christe*. The lectionary is then carried over to the celebrant who kisses it and says in a low voice: "Through the words of the Gospel may our sins be blotted out."

The deacon's position would depend on the location of the ambo, from which he would proclaim the sacred text. Custom dictates, however, that he stand at the left side of the sanctuary, facing the North, the place of cold and darkness, in which the light of the Gospel has not yet shone. Similarly, the celebrant of a private Mass also reads the Gospel on the left side of the altar, turning towards the North, with his hands joined like those of the deacon during a solemn Mass.

I believe in one holy, catholic and apostolic church.

XVI

THE HOMILY AND CREED

"By means of the homily, the mysteries of the faith and the guiding principles of the Christian life are expounded from the sacred text during the course of the liturgical year; the homily, therefore, is to be highly esteemed as part of the liturgy itself." (*Sacrosanctum Concilium*, no. 52.) In using this terminology, the conciliar constitution on the liturgy was merely recalling to mind a practice older than the Church itself. In fact, the homily was already and necessarily an integral part of the worship of the synagogue: "And Jesus entered the synagogue, according to his custom, on the sabbath day, and he rose up to read. And the book of Isaias, the prophet, was delivered unto him. And as he unfolded the book, he found the place where it was written: 'The Spirit of the Lord is upon me: wherefore he hath anointed.' And when he had folded the book, he restored it to the minister, and sat down. And the eyes of all in the synagogue were fixed on him. And he began to speak unto them" (Luke 4:16-21). Saint Paul goes on to do some of the same during his apostolic travels, and the first Christian assemblies will also be seen to have adopted such a practice: "When the reader has finished," writes Saint Justin in the midst of the second century, "he who presides over the gathering admonishes and challenges them to imitate these beautiful things."

Two things characterize the homily: it is a commentary on the readings and, being a liturgical act, it will usually be up to the celebrant to deliver it. It is not therefore a simple speech on the subject of God: it is truly an act of God Himself acting through the ministry of His Church.

In the early centuries of the Church, the bishop used to preach sitting from his throne situated in the depths of the apse, facing the assembly. This custom, inherited from the synagogue, emphasises the sacred, hierarchic aspect of the duty of preaching. For reasons of acoustics and convenience, the habit of standing while preaching has been adopted, either before the altar or from a pulpit situated in the nave.

With the *Credo*, we now come to the conclusion of the ante-Mass, or the Mass of the Catechumens. This hymn, full of authority and confidence is the assembly's response, in which they exclaim their adherence to the teachings contained in the homily. In Latin the Creed is sometimes called '*symbolum*', from the Greek *sumbolos*, which in antiquity signified "sign of recognition," or even "password." The *Credo* is in effect the 'password' of the Church militant: in order to be admitted to baptism, the catechumens must recite the '*symbolum*', after which they can effectively be counted among the disciples of the Lord. In the Christian life, there are two creeds in use: at Baptism and in daily prayers, the Apostles' Creed is used; at Mass, the later Nicene Creed is used. This latter one was a response to the heresies of Arius (on the divinity of the Word), and of Macedonius (on the divinity of the Holy Spirit). Henceforth, where the Apostles' Creed is content with saying: "I believe in Jesus Christ, His only Son," the later creed states: "We believe in one Lord, Jesus Christ, the only Son of God eternally begotten of the Father, God from God, Light from Light, true God from true God, begotten, not made, one in Substance with the Father."

The *Credo*, which only became part of the Mass in the fourth century to counter the above mentioned heresies, is reserved for certain occasions: on Sundays, and on the major feasts of Christ, the Holy Spirit, the Blessed Virgin, the Angels (*omnium invisibilium*), the Apostles (*apostolicam ecclesiam*), the saints (*ecclesiam sanctam),* and finally, the Doctors of the Church, who devoted their lives to handing on the Faith

Except at the words *et homo factus est*, where all kneel in honor of the Incarnation, the faithful remain standing throughout the *Credo*: the uprightness of their body acts as an image of the uprightness of their faith:

"We believe in one, holy, catholic and apostolic Church."

ABEL

The sacrifice of Abel (Mosaic in Ravenna)

THE OFFERTORY

In the same way as the priest receives from you that which he offers for you, so our Priest receives from us that which He offers for us: His flesh, in which He is made a sacrifice.

Saint Augustine

MAXIM

The Emperor Justinian carries his offering of bread to the altar. (Ravenna

XVII

The Offertory

The *Credo* having been recited, the Mass of the Catechumens now comes to an end. At this point, we begin what is called the Mass of the Faithful, or the Liturgy of the Eucharist. This properly sacrificial part of the Mass commences with the Offertory which is its first act.

At a solemn Mass, the deacon brings the following up to the altar: the **corporal,** a small white linen cloth which is stored within the **burse** and will be placed upon the central part of the altar where the host is to be laid, (the word 'corporal', then, comes from its association with the *Body* of Christ); and the **chalice**. During the Middle Ages, and until this day, on the occasion of a papal high Mass, the corporal would bear the dimensions of an actual table cloth covering the entire surface of the altar.

After this, the subdeacon, his shoulders covered by the humeral veil, brings up to the altar the **chalice,** the **paten,** and the **host,** which are covered by the **pall** (a small, square piece of cloth stiffened by a cardboard insert which will be used in covering the chalice so that nothing could accidentally fall into the Precious Blood), and another small cloth called a **purificator** with which the chalice is wiped and, at the end of Mass, the fingers of the priest who has handled the Body of Christ, after he has washed them. An acolyte accompanying the subdeacon will also bring two cruets, one containing wine and the other water.

The Matter of the Eucharistic Sacrifice.

Earlier in this book, it was explained that the sacraments consist of both matter and form. By the very fact that Christ Himself instituted the Eucharist, its matter is, under pain of invalidity, on the one part the bread of wheat, either without yeast according to the traditional usage of the Latin Church, or

73

leavened as it is sometimes done in the Orient; and on the other part, the natural wine of grapes: white according to modern usage in the West in order to avoid staining the altar cloths, or red, the color of blood, according to a more ancient usage preserved in certain countries; and a little bit of water.

There are three sacred vessels: the **paten**, which has the shape of a small plate, on which is laid the larger celebrant's host and, if there are just a few communicants, the smaller hosts which they are to receive; the **chalice**, in which the wine will be consecrated; and the **ciborium**, which is similar in appearance to a chalice, but also has a cover. Its purpose is to hold the smaller hosts which are destined for the members of the congregation who will receive Communion, and to store them in the tabernacle after Mass.

Traditionally all three vessels are to be made of gold, at least the interior. The chalice and the paten must be consecrated by the bishop, while the ciborium needs only to be blessed. The sacred vessels, as well as the sacred cloths (corporal and purificator) must be handled only by clerics or by lay sacristans who have been mandated by a priest to do so.

Throughout the first six centuries, the Offertory took the form of a long procession of the faithful bringing their personal offerings. These offerings were principally bread and wine which were destined to become the proper matter of the Sacrifice. Only the faithful brought offerings, however, because the catechumens, being dismissed by the deacon after the Liturgy of the Word and not yet counted among the members of Christ, cannot truly unite themselves to the offering of the Sacrifice. This procession is described in detail in the seventh century Papal Ceremonial: the pope, assisted by the archdeacon, receives the offerings from the nobility, while other clerics gather those of the people. Then, while the pope washes his hands, the offerings are divided into two parts: upon the altar are laid those which will be consecrated and, to one side, the surplus which will be distributed to the poor. This, therefore, is the origin of the custom (fairly widespread in France until quite recently) of bringing bread to Mass to have it blessed. Once it has been blessed by the priest, it is then

The offertory.

redistributed to the people at the church's doors when the Mass has ended.

In the Old Testament, this gesture of laying the offerings upon the altar is seen in itself to be a source of sanctification: "the altar shall be most holy; whatever touches the altar shall become holy" (Exodus 29:37). Therefore, simply laid upon the altar, the bread and the wine are already offered to God. However, other rites will bring this offering to a more perfect state, as will be shown later in this book.

The procession of offerings has survived in many ways. During the solemn Mass, the bread and the wine are not on the altar from the beginning of the Mass: it is only at the Offertory that the subdeacon and the acolyte, forming a sort of "mini procession," bring the bread and the wine to the altar on behalf of the people. In France in past years, some funeral Masses still retained the procession of the faithful who brought their (monetary) offering to the priest, who stood at the gate of the sanctuary. The collection which is taken after the homilies in our parishes today, as well as the Mass stipends which are offered to the priest beforehand, are the survival of this practice.

The meaning of this offering is easily perceived. First, the baptized individual intimately associates himself with the sacrificial act performed by the celebrant. This is why right after the Consecration, the priest says: "Wherefore, O Lord, we Thy servants (the priests), as also Thy holy people do offer unto Thy most excellent Majesty of Thine own gifts, bestowed upon us, a pure Host, a holy Host." Second, in bringing his offering, the baptized person offers himself: "It is necessary that when we accomplish the Sacrificial Act, we do immolate our own selves to God through the contrition of our hearts. Then, in fact, the host represents us before God, as if we ourselves have been made hosts." (Saint Gregory the Great, *Dialogues*, IV, 59.)

The Offertory procession which was used for many centuries in the Roman Mass was very soon accompanied by the chanting of a psalm, an expression of the sacred character of this offering, as well as its joyful character: "God loves a cheerful giver" (II Cor. 9:7). The Offertory antiphon of our Missal, which is sung by the choir or read by the celebrant, is a survival of this psalm.

Then the priest receives, from the deacon, the host on the paten, which is also a more recent development of the offering of the faithful: the priest offers that which he receives. Then, he lifts it up towards God in a gesture of offering, while saying: "Receive, Holy, Eternal and Almighty God, this immaculate host (from the Latin *hostia*, victim) which I ... offer for all the faithful living and dead, so that it may obtain for them, eternal salvation." One can notice that the host is already called an "immaculate victim." For the Byzantines, it is called the "Lamb." It is, therefore, right from the time of the Offertory, that the propitiatory sacrifice is being offered.

Some might object by saying that these Offertory prayers, unknown to the primitive Roman Mass, came to be only around the eight and ninth centuries. To this, one could answer that the offertory prayers of the Missal of Paul VI ("Blessed are you, Lord God of all creation. Through Your goodness we have this bread to offer, fruit of the earth and work of human hands. It will become for us the bread of life") date back only to earlier this century, and in relation to their ancestors, they are of a disconcerting poverty... There is good reason to regret the fact that the whole idea of a propitiatory sacrifice has been excluded from them.

Having offered the bread, the celebrant traces the sign of the cross on the corporal with the paten, at the very spot where he will lay down the host, because the Victim offers Himself on the cross.

The deacon, or in his absence the priest, pours the wine into the chalice. He then blesses the water just before pouring a little in the chalice. He blesses the water because it represents the faithful, who need to be purified before taking part in the sacrifice. (This explains why the water is not blessed at Masses for the dead, because it is no longer the faithful who we have in mind, but rather the souls in purgatory.)

The symbolism of the water mixed with the wine appears in the oration which the priest recites at this time: "May we be

The priest washes his hands.

absorbed in Christ as this drop of water is by the wine." In the Milanese, Lyonese, and the Carthusian Rites, a different prayer is said at this time, mentioning "the water and the blood which came out of the side of Christ for the remission of sins."

The celebrant then offers the chalice: "We offer Thee, Lord, the chalice of salvation. May it rise as a pleasing fragrance in the presence of Thy divine Majesty, for our salvation and that of the whole world." He then makes the sign of the cross on the corporal before placing the chalice upon it.

After two short prayers, the priest, at the solemn Mass, will incense the bread and the wine, which is a new sign of sacrifice and of offering. The prayer for blessing the incense brings to mind St. Michael the holy Archangel who stands at the right of the altar of incense, as well as all the elect: a new evocation of the great celestial liturgy, of which our earthly liturgies are a reflection.

In the Dominican Rite, the ceremonies of the Offertory are slightly anticipated, in that the preparation of the chalice is carried out before the reading of the Gospel.

Once the incensing is completed, the server pours water onto the priest's hands. Liturgists have always attributed a spiritual significance to this ablution. It is the gesture of an interior purification, without which man would not be able to stand before the altar of sacrifice. It can be found as early as in the book of Exodus (30: 19): "When they are to enter the Tent of Meeting they must wash in water for fear they die, and when they have to approach the altar for the service, to burn the offering burnt in honor of Yahweh."

Having returned to the center of the altar, the celebrant silently recites a last oration, the *Suscipe, sancta Trinitas?* (Receive, O Holy Trinity), which is like a summary of the whole Mass: a sacrifice which must be accepted by God, offered in memory of the Passion and the Resurrection, and uniting the Church on Earth with the Church in Heaven: "this oblation which we make to Thee in remembrance of the passion, resurrection and ascension of our Lord Jesus Christ, and in honor of blessed Mary ever Virgin, of blessed John the Baptist, the holy apostles Peter and Paul, of these and of all the saints: that it may avail to their honour and our salvation, and that they may be pleased to intercede for us in heaven, whose memory we now keep on earth: through the same Christ our Lord. Amen."

For this last silent supplication, as well as for the *In spiritu humilitatis*, the priest is slightly inclined before the altar. This is an attitude which was borrowed from the ceremonies of the king's court: one inclines himself in such a way when he is offering a gift to the king.

Having come to the threshold of mystery and conscious of his unworthiness, the priest turns towards the congregation and asks the faithful to pray for him, for it is for them that he will offer the sacrifice: *Orate, fratres,* "Pray, brethren, that my sacrifice and yours may be acceptable to God the Father Almighty."

Then, facing the altar, the celebrant again stretches out his arms towards Heaven while he prays the **Secret**, the prayer over the offerings. Throughout the first centuries, this was the only prayer for the whole of the Offertory. Like the Collect which concludes the entrance rituals and the Postcommunion which concludes those of the Communion, this prayer, the conclusion of the Offertory rituals, was also sung. Then, along with the beginning of the prayers said silently during the Offertory, it naturally came about that this oration also was said silently. This is the origin of the title of "Secret."

Generally, the Secret is a prayer which contains considerable theological density: terms such as *gifts, offerings, oblation, sacrifice, host,* and *victim* are constantly used. These gifts, present upon the altar, are offered to be consecrated into the sacrifice of Christ: "We offer Thee, Lord, these gifts which are destined to be consecrated."

Let us conclude with the Secret of Pentecost Monday, which summarises in a concise formula the whole theology of the sacrifice: "Sanctify these gifts in Thy goodness, Lord, we pray; receive the offering of this spiritual sacrifice and make of ourselves an eternal gift to Thee: through our Lord."

Dominican Rite:
preparation of the chalice (before the Gospel).

THE SACRED MYSTERIES

The solemn moment approaches, the priest raises his eyes and hands towards heaven, and enters, as it were, into the Holy of holies. There he speaks secretly to the Lord, in a grave and mysterious silence, so suited to this adorable sacrament.

Cardinal Bona

Missal of Mont-Saint-Eloi (13th cent.).

XVIII

THE CANON

The word *canon* is the literal transcription of the Greek word which signifies "rule."

Very early in the history of the Church, the Eucharistic Prayer was called *Canon Actionis* (rule of the Sacred Action), or *Canonica Prex* (ruled prayer), whence came the common usage of "Canon of the Mass." The Canon is the central part of the Mass, which reaches its highest point at the Consecration.

What is it that we call the "Consecration"? It is the moment in the Mass where, "by the words of Christ which the priest pronounces, acting *in the person of Christ,* the bread and the wine truly become the body and the blood of Christ." This is why the Consecration is considered to be the most sacred moment of the Mass.

Liturgical historians explain that during the first centuries the Canon also included the Preface. One of the oldest manuscripts of the Roman Mass, the Gelasian Sacramentary, bears these words before the dialogue of the Preface: *Incipit canon actionis.* If the Consecration is truly the heart of the Canon, it is easy to understand the need for such a solemn and majestic prelude, like a sacred arch through which we gain access to a mystery. That is in fact the function of the dialogue of the Preface: first, the usual *Dominus vobiscum* which precedes the prayer but which, this time, the celebrant sings without turning towards the faithful, because once the Sacred Action has begun he can no longer turn away from the altar. And while extending his hands towards Heaven, he adds *Sursum corda:* "Let us lift up our hearts!" To which the people answer with great enthusiasm, *Habemus ad Dominum,* "We lift them up to the Lord!" Then comes the thanksgiving (which is the meaning of the Greek word *eucharistia*): the priest bows and says *Gratias agamus Domino Deo nostro,* "Let us give thanks to the Lord our God." After the response of the people, the celebrant, with his hands raised up (as they will be throughout the Canon), intones: *Vere dignum et justum est, æquum et salutare,* "It is truly right and just, proper and helpful toward salvation." The Gregorian melody of the Preface, both sober and majestic, is truly a work of art. It is said that Mozart once exclaimed that he would gladly have sacrificed all of his accomplishments in exchange for the honor of having composed it himself. The Preface is, as it were, the first movement of the Eucharistic prayer: a great thanksgiving which Christ the Priest offers up to His Father, and which reaches its zenith in the hymn of the seraphim, the Sanctus, which unites the Earth to the Heavens in one common song of praise.

Following this great exultation comes silence: this is the second movement of the Eucharistic prayer, the "Canon" itself, the mystery which comes down from Heaven with a profound peace. Somewhat like the high priest of the Old Covenant, the celebrant detaches himself from the people and goes before the God of all holiness in order to offer Him the sacrifice: "Let all mortal flesh keep silence and stand with fear and trembling; and lift itself above all earthly thought. For behold the King of kings and Lord of lords, Christ our God, cometh forth to be our oblation." (Liturgy of Saint James). In the High Middle Ages the practice began of pronouncing the text of the Canon, those sacred and heavenly words *par excellence*, in a low voice so that not even the voice of the celebrant would break this sacred silence. The Carolingian liturgists bear witness to this fact, as they affirm that this practice of reciting the Canon in a low voice was introduced out of respect for the words which it contained, *ne verba tam sacra vilescerent,* so that words so holy would not be degraded.

What do the signs of the cross which the priest makes over the host and the chalice represent?

In the first place, they evoke the idea of a blessing. In this way, for example, the priest blesses the host before consecrating it when he says *benedixit.* However, according to liturgical historians, the primary purpose of these signs is actually to point to the offerings, while at the same time giving meaning to the words of the celebrant. Each time he mentions the oblations, the celebrant points to them in this way with the sign of the cross: before the Consecration, to call our attention to the mystery which will take place; but also afterwards, in order to encourage adoration of the holy species. He does not content himself with the simple gesture of the hand: as if to insist, and in order to recall the fact, that this Host is the victim of a sacrifice renewing that very one of Calvary, he uses the sign of the cross.

Why is it that these signs are so numerous?

Far from being excessive, the repetition of the gestures, of the rites, and of the words are characteristic of liturgical expression. The Church seeks to put itself in tune with the celestial liturgy: does the Book of Revelation not describe the four Living Beings "who incessantly repeat day and night: Holy, holy, holy, Lord, God, Master of All"? The great hymn which is punctuated with the prostrations of the twenty four Elders, indefinitely repeated: "And each time the Living Beings offer glory, honour and thanksgiving to Him who sits on the throne and who lives forever and ever, the twenty four Elders prostrate themselves before Him who sits on the throne, in order to adore Him who lives forever and ever." To declare these repetitions to be superfluous, would be a profound misconception of an elementary principle of liturgy: "The life of the liturgy does not consist in 'pleasant' surprises attractive attractive 'ideas', but in solemn repetitions" (Cardinal J. Ratzinger, *The Ratzinger Report,* Ignatius, 1985, p. 126).

Let us take note of the concern our Fathers felt in respecting even the smallest details in the celebration of the Mass. For example, at the beginning of the Middle Ages, Saint Boniface asked Pope Zachary, "In how many places, in the celebration of the Canon, must crosses be made?" and the Pope sent him a manuscript on which he had written the number of signs required.

Why does the priest extend his hands over the host and the chalice during the 'Hanc igitur' prayer?

It consists of a blessing gesture which is quite common in liturgy: the bishop confers priestly ordination by the imposition of the hands on the candidate, the ritual of baptism calls for not a few impositions of the hands on the cathecumen. The Middle Ages saw even more in this gesture, executed over the offerings of the Mass: it is a particularly evocative suggestion of the Old Covenant sacrifices. "Aaron," says Leviticus (16:20-22) concerning the scapegoat, "must lay his hands on its head and confess all the faults of the sons of Israel, all their transgressions and all their sins, and lay them to its charge. Having thus laid them on the goat's head, he shall send it out into the desert led by a man waiting ready, and the goat will bear all their faults away with it into a desert place." Could we have shown in a clearer way that the bread and the wine will become, in a few moments' time, the spotless Victim, the Lamb of God who bears the sins of the world?

Why does the celebrant look up towards heaven just before the Consecration?

The Evangelists report that our Lord often looked up towards heaven like this, especially in the most important moments of His life on Earth: in front of Lazarus' tomb (John 11:41); before healing the deaf mute (Mark 8:34); at the beginning of the sacerdotal prayer, just before His Passion: "He lifted up His eyes to heaven and said, 'Father, the hour has come; glorify thy Son that the Son may glorify thee.'" (John 17:1). But it is particularly the account of the multiplication of the loaves which especially bring to mind the gestures of the priest (Mark 6:41): "He looked up to heaven, and blessed, and broke the loaves." The priest, acting *in persona Christi* at the Mass, by looking this way towards heaven, expresses this profound and mysterious union between him and Christ, and between Christ and His Father.

The priest also lifts up his eyes up towards heaven at the beginning of the Canon, as well as at seven other times throughout the Offertory of the Mass.

What are the signs which manifest the respect that the Church has for the Consecration?

First of all, we must mention the Elevation of the Host. How did this practice come to be? Let us recall that the tenth century had been seriously shaken by the heresies of Berenger of Tours (d.1088), who denied the reality of the Consecration and of the Real Presence of Jesus Christ in the Eucharist. This crisis, along with the healthy reaction that it brought about among theologians and, indeed, the entire Church, strongly contributed to the focussing the attention of the faithful on the consecrated Host, the object of such controversies.

In this way, then, was born "the desire to see the Host," an extremely popular characteristic of medieval piety. In order to meet this desire of the Christian people, at the end of the twelfth century, a decree of the Archbishop of Paris, Eudes de Sully, prescribed that the celebrant should elevate the Host after the Consecration, *ita ut possit ab omnibus videri,* in such a way that It could be seen by all. This custom quickly spread throughout the whole of the Western Church. To prevent the celebrant from being burdened during the elevation of the Host and the chalice, the deacon or the server gently raises the back of the chasuble.

Where did the practice of holding torches around the altar during the Canon come from?

A decree from the Carthusians in the thirteenth century prescribed that at the early morning Mass, celebrated before the break of dawn, the deacon or the server would hold a candle behind the celebrant *ut corpus Christi possit videri,* so that the Body of Christ could be seen. This practice spread and developed, and there were prescribed either two, four, or as many as six torches to be held by clerics, thus forming a guard of honor around the altar. From thence also came the use of the supplementary candle which the server places on the altar at the beginning of the Canon in the Dominican Rite of the Mass.

Why does the celebrant genuflect after the Consecration?

Up until the end of the Middle Ages, the liturgy had only

three principle signs of adoration: the inclination, the genuflection on both knees, and the full prostration of the body on the ground. The genuflection which we know today, which consists of putting one knee to the ground and standing right back up, was for a long time a popular civil act of homage which was reserved for temporal princes. Also, at the beginning of the thirteenth century, the first sign of adoration by the celebrant was a profound inclination which manifested his respect for the accomplished miracle of transubstantiation (changing of the bread and wine into the Body and Blood of Christ). In the following century, the genuflection began to supplant the inclination, and from the end of the fifteenth century (a century before the Council of Trent), the Roman Missal adds a second genuflection, after the elevation of the Host, and it also prescribes the same after the consecration of the chalice.

What is the attitude to be adopted by the faithful after the Consecration?

The *Dialogus Miraculorum,* by Césaire of Heisterbach, reports that in 1201 Cardinal Guido, who had been the pope's legate, published the following decree in Colona: "At the elevation of the Host, let all the people in the church kneel at the sound of the little bell." This is the first time that this subject was ever brought up. However, such prescriptions rapidly spread to other areas. The common practice now is to kneel sometime before the Consecration, to incline oneself during the genuflections of the priest, and to keep one's eyes fixed upon the Host when it is elevated. At the beginning of the century, Pope Saint Pius X encouraged the faithful to do so by attaching indulgences to the recitation of the invocation "My Lord and my God!" to be said during the elevation. Let us also note the fact that since the beginning of the twelfth century, the elevation has also been announced by ringing the bells in the church tower during high Mass, so that those who were absent could also turn towards the church and adore the Lord present in His Sacrament, a custom which is still quite common in monasteries.

At what precise time must we kneel and stand during the solemn Mass?

The Missal of Saint Pius V, in the chapter entitled "Concerning the way to kneel, sit or stand during the Mass," only gives rubrics which are to be observed by the clergy who are present in choir. Generally, the faithful also follow these rubrics: to kneel after the chanting of the *Sanctus* (or simply at the ringing of the bell which precedes the Consecration), to remain kneeling during the Consecration, then to stand up until the Communion. On days of penance, however, such as during Lent (except on Sunday which is never a day of penance, because we commemorate the Resurrection of Our Lord), we remain kneeling throughout the entire Canon up to the *Agnus Dei*. However, there are some customs which vary slightly from one country to the next. In France, for many centuries the faithful have remained kneeling throughout the entire Canon, even during the solemn Mass on Sunday, and then stood for the *Pater*. For practical reasons, it is always better to respect local customs.

Why does the celebrant keep his thumb and index finger joined together after the Consecration?

It is a known fact that however small the particle of the consecrated Host, it is truly the body of Jesus Christ. Hence, every consecrated particle must be treated with the greatest respect: "Take great care to lose nothing! Tell me, if golden strands had been given to you, would you not hold on to them with the greatest care, seeking not to lose any of them? Will you not then take even greater care of an object which is even more precious than gold and precious stones, in order not to lose even a crumb?" (*Mystagogical Catechesis,* attributed to Cyril of Jerusalem, fourth century). So also, in order not to let any small particles which may have stuck to the fingers fall anywhere, the celebrant keeps them joined together from the Consecration right up until the moment when he purifies them after the Communion. It is also for this reason that if he has to lay his hands down upon the altar after the Consecration, he will always lay them down on the corporal.

Are not such precautions overexaggerated?

Even greater respect than this existed in the Middle Ages. It is known, for example, that during the eleventh century the monks of Cluny would keep the thumb and the index finger of each hand fully joined right from the moment following the washing of the hands at the Offertory, and therefore far before the Consecration, in order to prevent any profane contact from that moment until the time when they would be called to touch the Host.

What is the Minor Elevation?

The elevation which follows the Consecration (introduced during the thirteenth century) has the purpose, as we have seen, to render visible the holy species for the adoration of the faithful. The meaning of the Minor Elevation is entirely different. This is when the celebrant, while pronouncing the last words of the Canon, elevates the Host and the chalice for a short time, towards heaven. This gesture, which is one of the most ancient liturgical signs, is of the same nature as the slight elevation of the bread and of the wine during the Offertory: that which is elevated is hence offered to God. The Minor Elevation is thus of great importance: it is all of the Canon, and, through the Canon, all of the sacrifice of the Mass, which is here offered to the Blessed Trinity, in a gesture which in its simplicity is full of meaning. It is the achievement, or the apotheosis, of the Canon.

In this offering, however, the faithful are not excluded: as they have kept silent since the *Sanctus,* they are now invited here to unite themselves, to associate themselves fully with the holy sacrifice with an *Amen!* that should resound like the one which, as described by Saint Jerome, resounded throughout the Roman basilicas "like a celestial thunder."

XIX

The Text of the Canon

It was a common thing during the sixties to speak of the "faults," the "shortcomings," and the "obscurities" of the Roman Canon. As a result, a study of its various elements has now brought to light its antiquity (in the fourth century, the Canon was just about the same as it is today); its theological depth (the four ends of the sacrifice, which are very well expressed); its literary beauty; and finally, the seemless unity of its various parts.

Making our way into the mystery

This long prayer addressed to the Father begins with a petition: something of an extension of the Secret, the priest requests that these gifts and this sacrifice be accepted, which are offered for the Holy Church (*Te igitur*), and more particularly for the intention of certain faithful (*Memento*), which he dares to mention because of their communion with the Church of Heaven (*Communicantes*). Let us notice too, the beautiful listing of Saints mentioned in the *Communicantes*, groups in a certain rigorous hierarchical order: first the immaculate Virgin Mary; then Saint Joseph; then the twelve apostles; and finally, twelve martyrs. Among these last are found six pontiffs, two clerics, and four laymen.

Having arrived at the threshold of the Mystery, the priest prays once again to the Father for the members of His Church, requesting for them the grace of final perseverance (*Hanc igitur*). Then a specific plea is made in the request that the sacrifice might be accepted: May this offering become the Body and Blood of Jesus Christ, the beloved Son (*Quam oblationem*).

The Consecration

Protestants have often been amazed by the fact that the

words of consecration in the Canon were not taken literally from Holy Scripture. This is because they forget that Mass was celebrated well before the writing of the Gospels and Epistles, and that we are dealing with a pre-scriptural tradition. Moreover, the whole account of the institution of the Eucharist has received in the Canon a formulation which was intentionally done with much care, bearing in mind the particular goal of focusing on its eminently sacred character: "He took the bread into His holy and venerable hands, and, lifting up His eyes to Thee, O God, His almighty Father." The formula for the consecration of the wine, developed in a particular way, shows that the new covenant, sealed in the Blood of Jesus, is part of God's eternal plan. As for the *Mysterium fidei*, the central mystery of our faith, it is the Blood of God shed for the salvation of the world.

Development of the Sacrifice

This sacrifice recapitulates the whole work of salvation: the Passion, the Resurrection, and the Ascension of our Lord; and in His memory, we offer to the Father the pure, holy, and immaculate Host (*Unde et memores*). May He accept this Host as He accepted those of the just of the old covenant (*Supra quae*); and furthermore, may He deign to receive It on His heavenly altar, so that the Communion will fill us with heavenly blessings (*Supplices*). May the Lord also remember those who will not be able to take part in this sacrifice: our deceased brethren; may He grant them light and peace (*Memento*). Finally, to those who are consecrated to His service, and who recognize themselves to be sinners, may He grant them a place in the assembly of the Saints (*Nobis quoque peccatoribus*).

Praise of glory

The Canon comes to an end with two "doxologies." The first (*Per quem*) is in honour of Christ, through Whom the Father creates these gifts which we offer (Offertory), sanctifies them (Consecration), and then gives them to us (Communion). The second (*Per ipsum*) is trinitarian. As we have seen earlier, it is the majestic conclusion of the Canon.

Let us take another look at the Canon

Let us see in detail, first of all, how the four ends of the sacrifice (adoration, thanksgiving, propitiation, supplication) are given their proper place: The adoration (*latria*) is made quite manifest in the very beginning of the Canon with the chanting of the Preface: "Through Christ, the Angels praise Thy majesty, the Dominations adore it, the Powers revere it." The priest bows during the hymn of praise and adoration, "Holy, Holy, Holy, Lord, God of hosts! Heaven and earth are full of your glory," and bows profoundly (an attitude of adoration) at the *Te igitur* and during the *Supplices*. The innumerable genuflections of the celebrant (before each time he touches the sacred species), the rite of Consecration and the Elevation, all equally illustrate this aspect of adoration (*latria*) in the sacrifice of the Mass. The thanksgiving (*eucharistia*) also exists right from the Preface: *Gratias agamus:* "Let us give thanks to the Lord our God", *Vere dignum:* "Truly it is right and just to give Thee thanks always and everywhere, Lord, Holy Father, through Christ our Lord." What do we give thanks for? For the "blessed Passion, the Resurrection, the glorious Ascension" of the Son, for the work of our salvation, which is renewed in each Mass. The propitiatory sacrifice is often mentioned. This is the one which delivers us from sin: "they offer it to you for the salvation of their soul" (*Memento* of the living), "the chalice of my Blood, shed for the remission of sins" (Consecration), "graciously receive this offering from the whole of your family: deign to free us from eternal damnation" (*Hanc igitur*). As for the *impetratory* character (prayer of petition) of this sacrifice, it would be necessary to quote the whole Canon, for from beginning to end it suggests an ardent supplication: the two prayers beginning with '*Memento*', the *In primis* (prayer for the Church), the *Hanc igitur*, the *Nobis quoque,* etc.

The author of the Canon

It would be naive to expect to find an author for a text which has taken nearly six centuries to come to a quasi-definitive stage. There are, however, many "layers" of editing which can easily be distinguished:

A pre-Christian substratum: the lyrics of the Preface, as well as the dialogue which precedes it, give a sense of Jewish inspiration. The exclamation of the *Vere dignum et justum est!* resounded throughout the assemblies of the ancient democracy.

The narrative of the Last Supper, the Consecration, and the final doxology (in a form less developed than the one we actually know today), all put us into direct contact with the Church of the Apostles and the martyrs, the Church of the first saints.

It is generally held to be true, and is certain in some cases, that the editing of the Canon and the organizing of its parts were undertaken by popes such as Saint Sixtus II, Saint Damascus IV, Saint Leo the Great, Saint Gelasius V, and finally, Saint Gregory the Great, who gave us the Canon essentially as it is today.

Who is the author of the Canon? Simply speaking, it is the Church-the Church of the Apostles, of the martyrs, and of the saints. Also is it rightful that the "venerable Roman Canon," according to the happy expression of Father Gy, can also be called holy, and that it will forever remain the irreplaceable form, the most sacred and adequate expression of the Eucharistic Prayer of the Roman liturgy.

Communion at the conventual Mass at Le Barroux.

THE CONCLUSION OF THE SACRIFICE

Every time you eat this bread and drink this cup, you proclaim the death of the Lord until He comes.

St Paul

XX

THE PATER AND THE LIBERA

The last part of the Mass, which begins with the **Pater**, may be called the Communion cycle. But there is a tendency to consider the *Pater* as the climax of the Canon, which it immediately follows, rather than a preparation for Communion, from which it is still separated by the **Libera**, the breaking of the Host, the *Agnus Dei*, the kiss of peace and its preceding prayer, and finally, the two prayers the priest says quietly before taking Communion.

The ancient Fathers, however, understood the fourth request, "Give us our daily bread," as a reference to the Eucharist. Even before the *Pater* became an integral part of the rite of the Mass, it was often considered to be a personal preparation for Communion. "Why, asks Saint Augustine, do we say the *Pater* before receiving the Body and the Blood of Christ? For the following motive: if, as is likley with our fragile human nature, our spirit has brought forth some inappropriate thought, if our tongue has let slip some idle words, all of this is erased by the prayer of our Lord in these words: Forgive us our trespasses." In Hippo, it was the custom for all - priests and faithful - to strike their breast at the words *Et dimitte nobis debita nostra* ...

Who must say the *Pater* at Mass? Unlike in the Oriental usage (previously used throughout Gaul), in the Roman usage the celebrant recites it alone, as the high priest intercedes in the name of all. The faithful, however, join in by expressing the last request: *Sed libera nos a malo*. The Roman discipline has varied, however, throughout the last forty years in regard to this particular point: in 1958, Pope Pius XII authorized the faithful to recite the Pater with the priest during Masses which were not sung, an authorization which was then extended by Pope Paul VI for sung Masses as well.

By reason of the great respect which is owed to the "Lord's Prayer," we do not dare to say it (*audemus dicere*) except under divine injunction (*divina institutione formati*). We must remember also that the first generations of Christians did not reveal the *arcana,* the "mysteries," to the pagans. The catechumens, dismissed from the church after the readings of the Mass, did not hear the *Pater,* and would only learn about it some time after their baptism. Still today we have them recite it during the ceremonies of baptism: we verify, before making them Christians, that they have learned well and retained the Prayer of the Lord.

There is another hint of the supreme importance which is given to the *Pater* in the Mass: the celebrant prolongs its last words by the prayer of the *Libera,* a new request for purification before Communion. From the eleventh century on, the priest recited the *Libera* in a low voice. Following medieval symbolism, the commixture (immersion of a small piece of the Host into the chalice), representing the resurrection, is preceded by a series of three moments of silence commemorating the three days Christ was in the tomb: the silence of the Secret, that of the *Te igitur,* and that of the *Libera.*

Toward the end of this prayer, having said *Da propitius pacem,* the priest signs himself with the paten, kisses it, and then places it under the Host for the breaking. He kisses the paten at *Da propitius pacem* because it is Communion which is the source of our peace. Moreover, in the Dominican Rite, it is by permitting the deacon to kiss the paten that the celebrant gives him the peace (and not by an embrace, as in the Roman Rite).

XXI

THE BREAKING OF THE HOST
AND THE KISS OF PEACE

In the breaking of the Host, we find one of the gestures entrusted to us by our Lord Himself: "He took bread, blessed it, broke it and gave it to them" During apostolic times the Mass was simply called the breaking of bread (Acts 2:42). In order to remain faithful to the very gestures of our Lord, the breaking of the bread still remains an integral part of the rite of the Mass. The symbolism is rich: it is one and the same Victim that is shared among all the communicants, which in turn creates among them a communion of rare intensity: "The fact that there is only one loaf means that, though there are many of us, we form one single body because we all have a share in this one loaf." (1 Cor. 10:17). A second teaching must also not be forgotten, even though the Modernists have abused it: in the example of his Master, the Christian must share (let us rather say: share himself) in order to give of himself to others.

From this shared Host, the celebrant puts a small piece into the chalice: this is the commixture. The origin of this ritual brings out the importance of one of the essential characteristics of the Eucharist. In Rome around the year 700 the Pope would have a piece of the Host which was consecrated during his Mass brought to each of the bishops of the neighboring churches as a sign of unity and of belonging to his communion. The bishops who received it before celebrating their own Mass put it into the chalice before taking Communion. This is a very vivid expression of a truth which is so dear to the Church: the Eucharist is the *sacramentum unitatis*, the sacrament of unity, gathering all the priests (and through them, all the faithful) around the one shepherd. This custom has since fallen into the realm of history, but the ritual of commixture still remains; furthermore, in the East and during the Carolingian epoch in the West, we would see in this an evocation of the image of the Resurrection, through the reuniting of the Body and the Blood. This is most appropriate because in the Eucharist, it is truly the Body and Blood of the resurrected and glorious Lord which we receive.

Before letting the particle of the Host fall into the chalice, the celebrant makes three signs of the cross over the chalice while saying *Pax Domini sit semper vobiscum*, as a kind of invitation to exchange the kiss of peace. But there are two rituals which have come in after the *Pax Domini*: first, the chanting of the *Agnus Dei*, introduced by Pope St. Sergius I during the seventh century to accompany the breaking of the Hosts into the many pieces which were necessary for all who were to receive Communion; and second, the *Domine Jesu Christe,* which is silently recited by the celebrant.

The Eastern and Gallican usages place the kiss of peace before the Offertory, in order to remain faithful to the injunction of the Master: "So then, if you are bringing your offering to the altar and there remember that your brother has something against you, leave your offering there before the altar, go and be reconciled with your brother first, and then come back and present your offering" (Matthew 5: 23, 24). Very early on, the Roman usage (already established in the fifth century) placed it after the Canon and before the Communion, "so that," says Pope St. Innocent I, "in that place might be confirmed, by the kiss, all of what has been said and accomplished by the holy mysteries," as if to seal all that has gone before it.

XXII

THE COMMUNION

We have already shown that in the rituals and prayers which precede the Communion there is a reccurring theme: the unworthiness of the communicant and his repentance of his sins. The chant of the *Agnus Dei*, adopted by the Roman liturgy in order to accompany the 'breaking of the bread', is not an exception here: we strike our breast while responding *miserere nobis*. The kiss of peace is also a sort of illustration of the *sicut et nos dimittimus* of the Pater. Notice also the hierarchical aspect of the ritual kiss of peace: the priest and the deacon kiss the altar (which represent Christ, our true Peace), and only then do they exchange the kiss of peace, which will then be passed on to the clergy. In the days when men and women were kept separate in churches, they received and gave the kiss of peace in this way. The practice died out because of abuses which later began to creep in.

The Communion of the Priest.

Very early in the Church it became a prerogative of the celebrant to be the first to take Communion: "So that," said Theodore Mopsueste, "it might be made clear that it is he, according to the well defined rule of the priestly office, who has offered the sacrifice for all." Before taking Communion, the priest recites two prayers. The first (*Domine Jesu Christe, Filius Dei vivi*) is remarkable for its richness in theological content: the whole of redemption is alluded to (Christ, Son of God, has given life to the world by His death), as well as the fruits which we await from the sacrifice (deliverance from sin, faithfulness to the commandments, and final perseverance). The second prayer makes evident the unworthiness of the creature that makes him unable to approach Holy Communion except through the bountiful grace of the Lord (*pro tua pietate*).

Then comes the triple *Domine, non sum dignus*, which repeats the feelings of the preceding prayer, and where one strikes one's breast as a sign of compunction. These words of the centurion in the Gospel are also found in the Ethiopian and Byzantine Rites.

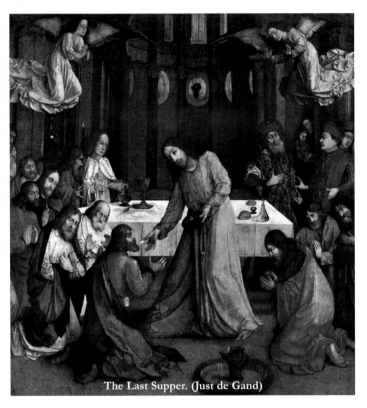

The Last Supper. (Just de Gand)

The Communion of the Faithful.

Given the fact that it is not strictly necessary for the integrity of the sacrifice, the Communion of the Faithful is nonetheless the normal outcome. Records of the early Church even indicate that deacons had the mission to take Communion to those who were absent. Very quickly, however, the Church had to come to terms with the lukewarmness of those assisting ("It is in vain," said Saint John Chrysostom, "that we go up to the altar: there is no one who comes to take part"); and later, with the growing respect which also had a tendency to keep the faithful away from the holy table. As a consequence, the councils established norms in regards to the obligations of the faithful toward the Holy Eucharist. The present discipline of the obligation to receive Easter Communion goes all the way back to the Fourth Council of the Lateran (1215).

The preparatory prayers of the faithful are the same as those of the celebrant (*Pater, Libera, Agnus Dei)* to which were added in the twelfth and thirteenth centuries the *Confiteor*, and, as a consequence of Protestantism, an act of faith in the true presence to be made by the communicant. This act of faith was later replaced in the sixteenth century by the celebrant's *Ecce Agnus Dei*, a profession of faith to which the faithful assent in their reception of Communion.

Without spending too much time on the subject, let us clarify, however, that if the Christians of the early centuries were in fact familiar with receiving Communion in the hand, receiving Communion in the mouth very soon became the preference (a council of Rouen in 878 forbade Communion in the hand for all the laity) seeing that it was more respectful, especially in regards to the smaller particles which stick to the hand and in this way might risk being profaned.

Communion under both species for the laity, although frequent in the early centuries, disappeared in the Middle Ages at about the same time when the doctrine of the integral presence of Christ in both species was defined. Since Christ is present in the Host by His Body, Blood, Soul, and Divinity, Holy Communion is the same whether received under one or both species. Communion by the chalice has survived, however, in certain very particular circumstances, such as the coronation of a king or the consecration of a bishop.

From Christian antiquity, the administration of the Eucharist has been accompanied by a short prayer. The most ancient is simply *Corpus Christi*, which is a true profession of faith to which the communicant associates himself by responding *Amen*. The prayer was expanded quite early on, as an illustration of the promise of our Lord (Whoever eats of this bread will live for ever): *Corpus Domini nostri Jesu Christi custodiat animam tuam in vitam aeternam*, to which the celebrant himself adds *Amen*.

The Communion Chant.

As in the entrance and the offertory processions, the communion procession is accompanied by the chant of a psalm, of which the Missal's communion antiphon is a type of survival. It expresses the joy and confidence of the Christian who is receiving his Lord: "Taste and see how good the Lord is; happy the man who takes refuge in Him" (Psalm 33, 8th Sunday after Pentecost).

The Ablutions.

After Communion, the celebrant proceeds to the ablutions. Let us describe in detail this ceremony, which today is not well known, in which is expressed the Church's great respect toward the Blessed Sacrament. The celebrant begins by scraping the corporal with the paten in order to gather up the particles of Host which might be found on the cloth. Then with his thumb and his index finger he makes them fall into the chalice, as well as those which could be found upon the communion paten which the server was holding in front of the communicants. The server then pours some wine into the chalice in order to dissolve any drops of the Precious Blood which remain, and to permit the priest to consume the small particles which he has gathered. Having taken this first ablution, the priest places over the chalice the extremities of his thumbs and index fingers, over which the server will pour wine and then water in order to remove the particles which might still be stuck to the celebrant's fingers. The priest also consumes this second ablution, so that not even a small particle of Host might be thrown out. Two short prayers accompany these rituals which really express the fruit which we hope for from Communion: purification of the smallest stain due to sin, and eternal life.

As in the rituals of the Entrance and the Offertory, those of the Communion are also brought to an end by a prayer, the

Postcommunion, which is said out loud by the celebrant in the name of the whole assembly. The faithful can benefit greatly from following the translation of it in their hand Missals, for at each Mass, in a concise prayer, it offers us a theme of thanksgiving which is doctrinally rich. "Grant us we beseech Thee, O Lord, to be filled with the eternal enjoyment of Thy Divinity, which is prefigured by the reception of Thy precious Body and Blood in this life." (Postcommunion of Corpus Christi).

Blessing of the people
(maronite rite)

XXIII

Ite, Missa Est

The Postcommunion having been sung by the celebrant, all that remains is to dismiss the congregation. But before that, the Roman liturgy calls down divine help and protection upon the people returning to their occupations: this is the role of the "prayer over the people" (*super populum*), which in the Missal of Saint Pius V was found only in the Masses of Lent, but which was included in every Mass prior to that time. Its particular character of blessing becomes clearly evident when it is preceded by the injunction given by the deacon, *Humiliate capita vestra Deo*, "Bow down your heads before God." After this final prayer, the deacon officially dismisses the congregation: *Ite, missa est*, "Go, you are sent". On days when a liturgical action immediately follows the Mass (a procession, for example), the dismissal is replaced by an invitation to give blessings to God: *Benedicamus Domino*.

Then the celebrant kisses the altar before leaving it as a sign of farewell. In the Syrian liturgy of Saint James, the sense of this last kiss is developed by the recitation of the prayer: "Remain in peace, holy and divine altar of the Lord! I do not know if it will be granted to me to come to you again. May the Lord grant that I may see you in heaven, in the Church of the first born." In the Roman Rite, the *Placeat* prayer which the celebrant says at this time evokes once again the dual sense of the sacrifice of the Mass and of all liturgy: the honour we give to the Divine Majesty, and the fruits which we receive from our participation.

The final blessing.

In descriptions of papal ceremonies we learn that around the middle of the eighth century, when the Pope had come down from the altar and was about to begin processing out after the *Ite, missa est*, the clergy and faithful present would come before him saying, *Jube domne benedicere* (Please bless us, sir). The Pope would bless them in this way: *Benedicat nos Dominus* (May the Lord bless us). When the use of the *super populum* prayer became less frequent, a blessing which is said out loud by the celebrant just before he leaves the altar was substituted in its place: *Benedicat vos omnipotens Deus, Pater, et Filius, et Spiritus Sanctus.* This is the formula in the Missal used today. At a private Mass, only one sign of the cross accompanied these words, but in the presence of a large congregation, the priest would make three signs of the cross in various directions over the faithful. This was in the rubrics of the Missal of Saint Pius V (1570), but Clement VIII reserved these three signs of the cross to the bishop only, a rule which is still kept today. Despite the integration of this blessing within the ritual of the Mass, the custom still remains for the bishop to bless the people as he processes out.

The Last Gospel.

At first sight the reading of the Last Gospel seems a bit incongruous at the end of the Mass (the readings apparently belonging instead in the first part of the Mass). This is, however, easily explained when we learn that it is also a certain kind of blessing. By reason of the profound mystery which it expresses, the prologue of Saint John enjoyed quite an extraordinary prestige in the early days of the Church. Many people would carry the text upon themselves, as some would a medal today, in order to obtain divine favours. At the beginning of the eleventh century, many faithful begged to hear it after Mass. The ceremonies of its recitation are not uniform: in the Roman Rite, the priest reads it at the altar, whereas the bishop recites it whilst leaving the altar, as does the priest in the Lyonese Rite. At private Masses during the Middle Ages, the Dominicans would say it while taking off their vestments, while the Carthusians never adopted the practice.

EPILOGUE

THE ROMAN MISSAL

During the sixth and seventh centuries, an era to which we owe the existence of the most ancient ancestors of the Roman Missal, namely the Sacramentaries, the framework of the Roman Mass was quite well established. During the Middle Ages, copies of these liturgical books gradually proliferated throughout Europe, and because of the great prestige of the Church of Rome, "mother and mistress of all the churches, *mater et magistra omnium ecclesiarum*," they came to supplant the local liturgical books. At the same time, the Roman Rite adopted many features of these local rites, leading to the formation of a mixed "Romano-Franco" Missal. This Missal, supplanting the "pure Roman" one, even in Rome, went on to become, under Pope Innocent III, the Missal "according to the usage of the Roman curia". This Missal was adopted by the greatly flourishing order of Saint Francis, and so soon spread throughout Europe.

In order to remedy the problem of anarchy in which the liturgy found itself in many dioceses during the fourteenth century, the Council of Trent charged the Pope with the responsibility of producing an edition of the Roman Missal for the whole Latin Church. Saint Pius V therefore had the Missal "according to the usage of the Roman curia" reprinted with hardly any changes. When the bishops received the Missal "of Saint Pius V," there were no surprises, for they were already quite familiar with this liturgy, which hardly differed from the older diocesan Missals they had previously been using for a long time.

In this way, almost every diocese of France adopted the Tridentine Roman Missal of 1570. Since then, many editions have followed with few additions (which shows that the traditional liturgy has remained alive): Masses of newly

115

canonized saints, modifications of some details in the ritual of the Mass (such as the manner of making inclinations, the number of prayers to say at each Mass, days on which to say the *Gloria* or the *Credo*...). The most recent edition is that of 1962, which is used by priests and communities that still celebrate the Holy Sacrifice of the Mass according to the "classical Roman rite," to employ that very joyful expression of Cardinal Ratzinger's.

Without raising protests against the prerogatives of the Holy See in regard to liturgical reform, and without being partial, it would seem that the Missal which came about after Vatican II, given the extent of the changes which were introduced, has seen a kind of rupture with this lineage. Father Robert Amiet, an eminent specialist in the realm of the history of liturgical books, notes in the following comment, which is taken from the preface of his catalogue *Missels et bréviaires imprimés* (Printed Missals and Breviaries): "Personally, I have advanced this limit (in cataloguing the editions of the Roman Missal) to 1970, a date at which the liturgical transformations which were brought about by the Second Vatican Council brutally and definitely served to abolish the ancient liturgy, one which had been inaugurated by Charlemagne, and which had endured, in good times and in bad, almost twelve centuries."

Is that, then, the final word? The present Holy Father has happily given us the assurance of the opposite:

"Moreover, respect must everywhere be shown for the feelings of all those who are attached to the Latin liturgical tradition, by a wide and generous application of the directives already issued some time ago by the Apostolic See, for the use of the Roman Missal according to the typical edition of 1962" (*Motu Proprio* "Ecclesia Dei adflicta", 7.).

Unfortunately, we have not quite yet arrived at the "wide and generous application," but does the last word not belong to the virtue of hope?

PHOTO CREDITS

Cover, 53, 82, 92: Abbaye Saint-Madeleine du Barroux; 8: *The Last Judgement* (detail), Bl. Fra Angelico; 10: *The Holy Sacrifice of the Mass*, Atelier de la Saint Espérance; 16: Photo by Fortier; 15: Photo by Andersen; 28: Ivory diptych (Frankfurt); 27 & 66: Photos by Kessel; 45: Photo by Morath; 51: Photo by Scala; 60: Photo by Enit; 64: Photo by R. G. Phelipeaux; 70 & 72: Photos by Alpina; 75 & 78: Photos by Abbaye Sainte-Marie de La Pierre-qui-Vire; 81: Photo by Solia; 90: *The elevation of the Host*, Andrea Pisano (Florence, campanile of the Cathedral); 100: Communion procession (Abbaye Sainte Madeleine), photo by Alain Licheron; 112: photo by Decker.